Computing Natural Language Inference Workshop 2017

Montpellier, France
19 – 22 September 2017

ISBN: 978-1-5108-5285-3

Printed from e-media with permission by:

Curran Associates, Inc.
57 Morehouse Lane
Red Hook, NY 12571

Some format issues inherent in the e-media version may also appear in this print version.

Printed by Curran Associates, Inc. (2017)

Association for Computational Linguistics
209 N. Eighth Street
Stroudsburg, Pennsylvania 18360

Phone: 1-570-476-8006
Fax: 1-570-476-0860

acl@aclweb.org

Additional copies of this publication are available from:

Curran Associates, Inc.
57 Morehouse Lane
Red Hook, NY 12571 USA
Phone: 845-758-0400
Fax: 845-758-2633
Email: curran@proceedings.com
Web: www.proceedings.com

TABLE OF CONTENTS

Incrementality all the way up

Ellen Breitholtz, Christine Howes, Robin Cooper
University of Gothenburg, Sweden
ellen.breitholtz@ling.gu.se, christine.howes@gu.se, robin.cooper@ling.gu.se

September 5, 2017

A major challenge in formal analysis of discourse is that inferential connections between different parts of a text or dialogue are usually not logical in the technical sense. Instead they are based on knowledge (or beliefs) which are assumed to be shared between the agents involved in the discourse. Because of its interactive nature, allowing for feedback, clarification requests, etc. inference in dialogue may be even harder to describe formally. It is well known that language, in particular dialogue, is incremental at phonetic, syntactic and semantic levels. In this paper we will take a closer look at incremental interpretation of reasoning in dialogue. Our approach takes rhetorical reasoning as its point of departure and utilises some key concepts from classical rhetoric. We also suggest a way of analysing rhetorical arguments in dialogue using an information state update approach cast in Type Theory with Records, that will allow us to represent how dialogue participants draw inferences incrementally, that is tentatively make an inference, and then recompute it in the light of more specified information.

In (1) we see an example of how a dialogue participant interprets language incrementally. Following A's production of the noun phrase (NP) 'the doctor', i.e. before there is a complete proposition to interpret, B clarifies who is being referred to by A, thus indicating that for B, the referent of the NP is underspecified at this point in the exchange. Note that B could have produced a backchannel ('mm') here instead of the clarification request (CR), in which case we would not know whether or not the NP was underspecified for B – B may have correctly identified the specific doctor 'Chorlton' as the intended referent, or B might not have cared who the doctor was.

(1)
1. **A:** Er, the doctor
2. **B:** Chorlton?
3. **A:** Chorlton, mhm, he examined me ... [BNC: KPY 1006-1008]

Just as people are able to make low level interpretations incrementally from incomplete information, as in (1), we propose that higher level interpretation in dialogue is also incremental.

As illustrated in example (1), one of the key ways that we can investigate the incrementality inherent in dialogue is by examining examples of miscommunication. Miscommunication is often taken as something to be avoided in dialogue, as participants strive to align their mental representations with one another (Pickering and Garrod, 2004). However the local resolution of (potential) miscommunication at all levels is key in driving dialogue forward.

Examples of visible miscommunication also illustrate that interpreting what we have been given as early as possible means that incremental processing is non-monotonic. In example (1), B has offered a (tentative) fully specified interpretation in the CR ('Chorlton?'), but of course, this could be rejected by A (by saying e.g. "no, Fitzgerald"). In this case, B's initial interpretation is incompatible with A's subsequent turn, and will have to be abandoned and the new interpretation assimilated. Such mismatches can also occur in the reasoning undertaken by dialogue participants.

In example (2), we can see how one argument may be interpreted differently by two dialogue participants depending on the underpinning reasoning (topoi) they assume the argument to be based on. This is possible since arguments in dialogue are usually *enthymematic* i.e. drawing on tacit premises and principles of reasoning.

This kind of mismatch may go unnoticed in cases where consensus is reached. After all, if the interlocutors agree on the conclusion of the argument there is often no reason to argue about the rationale for agreeing. However, in example (2) it is made explicit that the speaker and the listener interpret the enthymeme in (2a) drawing on different topoi.

(2) a. **P:** Metal was actually the reason I started doing hip hop.

b. **P:** ... Because I hated metal

c. **J:** Oh, I thought you were going to say something completely different!

This snippet of dialogue is taken from a radio program where Swedish hip hop artist Petter is asked of his opinion of a song that has just been played. The example (2) demonstrates that incrementality in interaction concerns not only phonetic, syntactic and semantic aspects of language, but also pragmatic inferences. We propose a model to account for this using the notion of *underspecified* enthymemes (Breitholtz, 2014), illustrated using example (2).

Although great progress has been made over the past decade in the semantics and pragmatics of dialogue, some issues remain unsolved. One common problem for approaches to dialogue modelling is that they have an impoverished notion of context, since they are extensions of models developed to account for the truth value of sentences in terms of possible worlds rather than the meaning of utterances in interaction. There are, however, exceptions to this. By employing *information state* models of language (Ginzburg, 2012; Larsson and Traum, 2000) it is possible to account for how coordination of the dialogue gameboard (DGB) progresses with successive utterances. The DGB provides a structured characterisation of the information available to dialogue participants and offers a principled way in which asymmetries in shared knowledge can be represented. A common denominator for recent work along these lines (Ginzburg, 2012; Breitholtz, 2014; Cooper and Ginzburg, 2015) is that it uses Type Theory with Records (TTR) (Cooper and Ginzburg, 2015). TTR is based on the idea that humans perceive the world in terms of categories or *types*. In order to represent complex situations, TTR employs *record types*. A record type is a structure of pairs of labels and types where a label is like a variable associated with a type, e.g. individual (entity) and ptype (a type of situation constructed from a predicate and appropriate arguments).

The record types of TTR are used to model situation types and enable us to include virtually any feature from semantic context to phonology in our characterisation of a situation type, which makes TTR particularly well suited for modelling dialogue, where factors like context and intonation are often essential. Moreover, the notion of subtyping in TTR makes it possible to represent how a dialogue participant's take on the situation is incrementally built up during the course of a conversation. Record types offer a convenient way of doing this since we can easily add and remove fields, making a type more or less specified. Manifest fields in record types involve a restriction of the type in the field to a singleton type of one particular object of the type, thus enabling incremental partial specification of a record. TTR is also used by Purver et al. (2010); Eshghi et al. (2012) where it is combined with Dynamic Syntax (DS) (Kempson et al., 2001), an action-based grammar formalism which models the word-by-word incremental processing of linguistic input. In work by Breitholtz (2014); Breitholtz and Cooper (2011) dialogue semantics in TTR has been extended to include pragmatic reasoning, taking its point of departure in the Aristotelian concept of *enthymeme*. An enthymeme is an argument which relies on the listener supplying background knowledge or contextual information to correctly interpret the argument. If a dialogue participant presents the argument P therefore Q, the interlocutor must supply a warrant that P is a valid reason for Q in order for the argument to be successful. The supressed principles of reasoning (such as P implies Q in the example above) warranting enthymemes are referred to as topoi (Aristotle, 2007; Ducrot, 1988). When we interact we expect topoi to be common ground, or to be accommodated (adopted by dialogue participants) during the course of the interaction.

The speaker typically assumes that the topos accessed by other conversational participants to interpret an argument is similar to that which the speaker himself has in mind. However, sometimes our individual takes on the conversation as well as the state of affairs in general, do not match. As previously discussed agents involved in dialogue may accommodate different topoi which all satisfy the criteria for underpinning a particular enthymeme, while not being the ones assumed by the speaker. Although dialogue participants may have access to different topoi, and different topoi may be selected to plug into an enthymeme, it is not the case that the choice of topoi is entirely random or unpredictable. It is, however linked to situational context, domain and sociocultural context.

Before we have a look at the example of incremental reasoning in (2), let us consider (1) again, where the dialogue participants are incrementally specifying the interpretation of the noun phrase *the doctor*. In (3) we see the types of B's take on the concept at different points in the dialogue. First, the type B believes to be shared is that in (3a), where all that is specified is that the referent is a doctor. At the type of (3b) B has learnt, by means of a clarification question, that the doctor is Chorlton. At the type of (3c) B has also integrated the information that Chorlton was the one who examined A.

$$(3)\quad (a)\ \begin{bmatrix}\text{x:}\mathit{Ind}\\ \text{c:doctor(x)}\end{bmatrix}\qquad (b)\ \begin{bmatrix}\text{x=chorlton:}\mathit{Ind}\\ \text{c:doctor(x)}\end{bmatrix}\qquad (c)\ \begin{bmatrix}\text{x=chorlton:}\mathit{Ind}\\ \text{c:doctor(x)}\\ \text{c}_1\text{:examined(x,B)}\end{bmatrix}$$

A similar case regarding the incremental narrowing down of possible referents for proper names modelled in TTR can be found in Cooper (2017). We will now move on to see how we may model higher level incremental processing in a compatible framework.

P's first utterance in (2a) – "metal was the reason I started doing hip hop" – constitutes an enthymeme – there is *something* about metal that made Petter start doing hip hop. We represent enthymematic inference and topoi on the DGBs of dialogue participants as dependent types, i.e. functions from situations to situation types. Thus the enthymeme conveyed in Petter's first utterance can be represented as a function from a situation where metal occurs to a type of situation of a type where P starts "doing hip hop", as seen in (4). We refer to this enthymeme as $\mathcal{E}_{reason}$.

$$(4)\quad \mathcal{E} = \lambda r\text{:}\ \begin{bmatrix}\text{T=music:}\mathit{Type}\\ \text{x=metal:T}\\ \text{z=Petter:}\mathit{Ind}\\ \text{c}_1\text{:relevant(T)}\end{bmatrix} \cdot \begin{bmatrix}\text{y=hiphop:}r\text{.T}\\ \text{c}_2\text{:do(r.z,y)}\end{bmatrix}$$

$$(5)\quad \mathcal{T}_{similar} = \lambda r\text{:}\ \begin{bmatrix}\text{T:}\mathit{Type}\\ \text{x:T}\\ \text{z:}\mathit{Ind}\\ \text{c}_1\text{:relevant(T)}\\ \text{c}_2\text{:like(z, x)}\end{bmatrix} \cdot \begin{bmatrix}\text{y:r.T}\\ \text{c}_3\text{:do(r.z, y)}\end{bmatrix}$$

There might be several topoi accessible to J which would underpin the enthymeme $\mathcal{E}$. Judging from J's utterance she is surprised by P's assertion that he hated metal. This example shows that J begins to reason about P's assertion even before the second utterance. We claim that J accesses a topos to apply to the enthymematic argument as early as possible, which later must be abandoned in light of (2b). It seems reasonable to assume that J expected metal being the reason for P to do hiphop to be due to him liking metal. Thus, a possible topos could be one saying that if two activities are of the same type, and the speaker likes one of them, that may cause him to engage in the other activity. We see a formalisation of this topos, $\mathcal{T}_{similar}$ in (5).

Update rules for introducing rhetorical features onto the shared dialogue gameboard are presented in previous work (Breitholtz, 2014). Here we will not go into the formal details of these, but provide an informal account of the updates involved.

The basic principle for integrating a topos on the shared DGB is that the enthymeme first on the list of shared enthymemes[1] justifies the loading of a topos onto the shared gameboard if the enthymeme is a *specification* of the topos. This is defined as the antecedent part of the enthymeme being a subtype (less specific or identical to) the corresponding part of the topos. Secondly, the result of applying the enthymeme to a record r must be a subtype of the result of applying the topos to the same record. In other words: if you hear an argument and you are aware of a more general principle of which this argument is a case, you will interpret the argument in accordance with that principle.

In the case of $\mathcal{E}_{reason}$ (4) the antecedent type is *not* a subtype of the antecedent type of $\mathcal{T}_{similar}$ (5) since it lacks the constraint c_2: like(z, x). However, since dialogue participants sometimes do accom-

[1]Following Ginzburg's terminology for questions under discussion Ginzburg (2012) p. 68-69, we refer to this as "max eud".

modate topoi based on underspecified enthymemes, our model should be able to integrate topoi based on less strict requirements. Thus, if a dialogue participant hears an argument for which he is not aware of any more general underpinning warrant, he might coerce an interpretation based on a topos that is a more specific version of the enthymeme in the discourse.

The type of J's information state following the integration of $\mathcal{T}_{similar}$ (5) is shown in (6).

(6)
$$\left[\text{shared:}\begin{bmatrix}\text{eud=[}\mathcal{E}_{metal\_reason}\text{]:list(}\textit{Enthymeme}\text{)}\\ \text{topoi=[}\mathcal{T}_{similar}\text{]:list(}\textit{Topos}\text{)}\end{bmatrix}\right]$$

After P's second utterance in (2b) – "Because I hated metal" – a new enthymeme, $\mathcal{E}'$ (7), is integrated at the top of the list of enthymemes under discussion.

(7)
$$\mathcal{E}' = \lambda r\text{: }\begin{bmatrix}\text{T:}\textit{Type}\\ \text{x=metal:T}\\ \text{c}_1\text{:relevant(T)}\\ \text{z=Petter:}\textit{Ind}\\ \text{c}_{hate}\text{:hate(z, x)}\end{bmatrix} \cdot \begin{bmatrix}\text{y=hiphop:}r\text{.T}\\ \text{c}_2\text{:do(}r\text{.z,y)}\end{bmatrix}$$

(8)
$$\mathcal{T}_{l\_t\_e} = \lambda r\text{: }\begin{bmatrix}\text{T:}\textit{Type}\\ \text{x:T}\\ \text{y:T}\\ \text{z:}\textit{Ind}\\ \text{c}_1\text{:relevant(T)}\\ \text{c}_2\text{:hate(z, y)}\end{bmatrix} \cdot \begin{bmatrix}\text{e:start\_doing(r.z, r.x)}\end{bmatrix}$$

In this case the topos available seems to be incompatible with the enthymeme: $\mathcal{E}'$ says that since Petter hated metal, he started doing hip hop, and the topos $\mathcal{T}_{similar}$ says that if someone likes something s/he might start doing something similar. The antecedents include concepts that we would want to model as mutually exclusive, namely *like* and *hate*. Following Cooper (prep) we say that if T_1 = hate(x,y) and T_2 = like(x,y), T_1 precludes T_2, that is, no situation can be of both types.

In conversation we normally try to interpret underspecified or implicit content by drawing on information already introduced on the dialogue gameboard. However, when J realises the mismatch between the integrated topos $\mathcal{T}_{similar}$ (5) and the new enthymeme in (7), she searches her rhetorical resources (part of her long term memory) for a topos which could be drawn on to underpin $\mathcal{E}'$.

A topos that would work here would be one capturing the notion of "the lesser of two evils", $\mathcal{T}_{l\_t\_e}$ (8). The idea of this topos is that in a particular context or situation if you have two things to choose from, and one is bad, you pick the other one.

We have shown how a dialogue participant sets about interpreting an enthymematic utterance by trying to access a topos that may serve as underpinning for the enthymeme. We saw how dialogue participants can start reasoning before an argument is fully spelled out, in that there is a topos that warrants the enthymeme by being a generalised version of it. This indicates that the way we process rhetorical structure is analogous to the way we process sentential and non-sentential utterances as described in e.g. Eshghi et al. (2015) – by incrementally constraining the search space.

We can thus see how the pervasive incrementality at all levels of dialogue is also apparent in accessing the resources required for higher-level processes, i.e. reasoning.

We intend to continue this line of work, in particular in investigating to what degree underspecified enthymemes are actually used. Intuitively, in situations where dialogue participants know each other very well and/or the context allows it, they may infer topoi based on underspecified enthymemes, which turn out to be exactly the ones intended by the speaker. Furthermore, as with the possibility of repair at all levels of interaction, the possibility of asking follow up questions may make it efficient to reason based on underspecified enthymemes. We also plan to conduct a series of experiments to investigate the enthymemes people use in a dialogue, and to see what factors influence which argument people choose when more than one topos is available. This would also be a way of determining to what degree a particular topos is actually established in a particular dialogue.

References

Aristotle (2007). *On Rhetoric, a theory of civic discourse.* Oxford University Press.

Breitholtz, E. (2014). *Enthymemes in Dialogue: A micro-rhetorical approach.* Ph. D. thesis, University of Gothenburg.

Breitholtz, E. and R. Cooper (2011). Enthymemes as rhetorical resources. In *SemDial 2011 - Proceedings of the 15th Workshop on the Semantics and Pragmatics of Dialogue (LosAngelogue)*, pp. 149–157.

Cooper, R. (2017). Proper names in interaction. In S. Kurahashi, Y. Ohta, S. Arai, K. Satoh, and D. Bekki (Eds.), *New Frontiers in Artificial Intelligence: JSAI-isAI 2016 Workshops, LENLS HAT-MASH, AI-Biz, JURISIN and SKL Kanagawa, Japan, November 14–16, 2016, Revised Selected Papers*, Number 10247 in Lecture Notes in Artificial Intelligence, pp. 5–18. Springer.

Cooper, R. (in prep). Type theory and language: from perception to linguistic communication. Draft of book chapters available from `https://sites.google.com/site/typetheorywithrecords/drafts`.

Cooper, R. and J. Ginzburg (2015). Type theory with records for natural language semantics. In S. Lappin and C. Fox (Eds.), *The Handbook of Contemporary Semantic Theory*, pp. 375–407. Wiley.

Ducrot, O. (1988). Topoï et formes topique. *Bulletin d'études de la linguistique française 22*, 1–14.

Eshghi, A., J. Hough, M. Purver, R. Kempson, and E. Gregoromichelaki (2012). Conversational interactions: Capturing dialogue dynamics. In *From Quantification to Conversation*, Volume 19 of *Tributes*, pp. 325–349. College Publications.

Eshghi, A., C. Howes, E. Gregoromichelaki, J. Hough, and M. Purver (2015). Feedback in conversation as incremental semantic update. In *Proceedings of the 11th International Conference on Computational Semantics*, London, UK.

Ginzburg, J. (2012). *The Interactive Stance: Meaning for Conversation.* Oxford University Press.

Kempson, R., W. Meyer-Viol, and D. Gabbay (2001). *Dynamic Syntax: The Flow of Language Understanding.* Blackwell.

Larsson, S. and D. Traum (2000). Information state and dialogue management in trindi dialogue move engine tool kit. *Natural Language Engineering 6*, 323–240.

Pickering, M. and S. Garrod (2004). Toward a mechanistic psychology of dialogue. *Behavioral and Brain Sciences 27*, 169–226.

Purver, M., E. Gregoromichelaki, W. Meyer-Viol, and R. Cann (2010). Splitting the 'I's and crossing the 'You's: Context, speech acts and grammar. In *Proceedings of the 14th Workshop on the Semantics and Pragmatics of Dialogue*, Poznań, pp. 43–50.

Quantifier Scoping and Semantic Preferences*

Davide Catta
LIRMM, Université de Montpellier
davide.catta@lirmm.fr

Mehdi Mirzapour
LIRMM, Université de Montpellier
mehdi.mirzapour@lirmm.fr

Abstract

This paper addresses the problem of ranking valid semantic readings of a given multiple-quantifier sentence. The proposed model is based on extending Morrill's account on the syntactic complexity profiling of the categorial proof-nets. The extension uses some techniques that are inspired by Hilbert's epsilon operator and the syntactic structure constraints. Our preferential model on different semantic readings can potentially be integrated into natural language inference systems.

1 Introduction

The ultimate goal of this research is to rank valid semantic meanings of a given multiple-quantifier sentence that can be gained from both syntactic and semantic representations; and for the time being, without taking into account other possible factors such as common sense and lexical knowledge.[1]

The described problem is not purely a theoretic one; it is raised with the intention of application in the project e-fran AREN (ARgumentation Et Numerique) for the automated analysis of online debates by high-school pupils. The syntactic formalism that is used in the project is categorial grammars which are suitable for deriving meanings as the logical formulas. Grail (Moot (2017, 2012)), an automated theorem prover is used for parsing. It relies on a chart-based system close to categorial natural deduction which can rather smoothly be transformed to proof-nets.[2] The problem of ranking the possible readings can be tackled if we employ the existing techniques that use proof-nets for measuring the complexity of readings (Morrill (2000); Johnson (1998)). We are specifically interested in Morrill's approach, but as we will see adopting this technique to our problem is not as straightforward as it seems. Our goal in this research is to fix theses issues and improve Morrill's technique for the representing and ranking semantic ambiguities for multiple-quantifier sentences.

Since sentences with quantifier scope ambiguities often have two (or more) non-equivalent semantic readings, capturing these phenomena with some plausible ranking techniques can potentially be useful for natural language inference systems. It is worth mentioning that different readings allow different inference paths and as it is shown in some studies (Durand-Guerrier (2016)) we can trace back the root cause of some *invalid inferences* in the misinterpretation of quantifiers as when occurs in quantifier scoping phase.

*This work is partially supported by the e-fran project AREN (ARgumentation Et Numrique) for the automated analysis of online debates by high-school pupils.

[1] For a historical survey on this topic see chapter "The Natural History of Scope" in Steedman (2012).

[2] Two important features of the AREN project: (i) since, the data are provided in written language by the high-school pupils, we do not need to model intonation and prosody as a cue for disambiguation. (ii) there are, on average, 20 words in each sentence with almost two hundred category types, and the replies of the users happen with some delays. This restriction makes our solution scalable for this specific project that does not demand any big data analysis. Hence, it does not raise the issues of real-time processing and complexity.

2 Advantages and Drawbacks of the Morrill's Approach

A proposal is put forward (Morrill, 2000, p.333) which works very well for a wide variety of performance phenomena such as garden-pathing, the unacceptability of center embedding and preference for lower attachment. It works in Lambek categorial grammar framework (Lambek (1958), (Moot and Retoré, 2012, Chapter 2)). The measurement uses syntactic analysis represented in the proof-net structure and gains the complexity profile by counting the number of unresolved dependencies of each word. This measurement is supposed to represent, in a numerical way, the course of memory load in optimal incremental processing. Formally speaking, we can rewrite Morrill's definition as follows: let $s = w_1, \cdots, w_n$ be a given sequence of words with n size, and let $R_1, \cdots, R_m$ be m number of categorial proof nets that represent all the possible (cut-free) semantic readings of s. We can define a function f_{cm} from $P = \{R_1, \cdots, R_m\}$ to $\mathbb{R}$ that maps R_i to the inverse of the sum of unresolved valencies before and after each root in R_i. We can say $R_i >_m R_j$ (read as R_i is Morrill-preferred to R_j) iff $f_{cm}(R_i) > f_{cm}(R_j)$.

There are two general objections against this approach. The first objection comes back to the choice of Lambek categorial grammar which simply can not derive all valid semantic readings. We address this objection in section (3.2) by providing a complexity measuring technique that works only on the valid readings, and not over-generated readings that exists in the storage-based techniques (Cooper (1983), Keller (1988)). The second objection, which is more important than the first one, is that Morrill's approach simply fails in some examples such as utterances that have sentence-modifier adverbials, nested sentences or direct speech. We can consider the following sentences:

(1) Everyone repairs something expertly.[3]
(2) "Someone loves everyone", said John.

Figure 1: Categorical Proof-nets and Complexity Profile for Example (1)

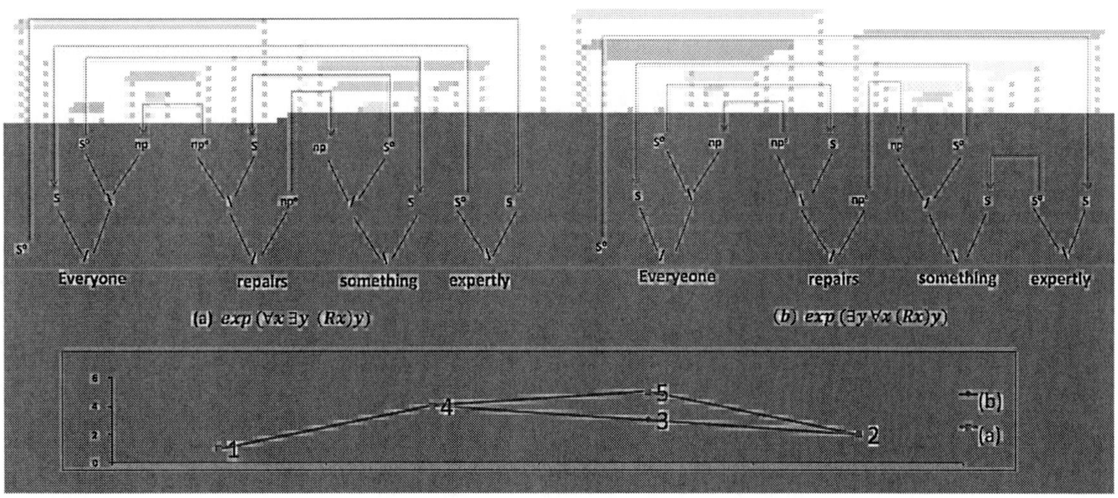

Figure (1) illustrates two corresponding proof-nets and complexity profiles for the example (1)– the reader can verify the example (2) for herself. As it is shown, the Morrill's criteria for choosing the left-to-right preference fails, since the reading (a) which is supposed to have lower complexity is predicted

[3]Thanks to one of the reviewers that pointed up the distinction between VP-oriented adjunct and Clause-oriented adjunct as it is indicated in (Huddleston et al., 2002, p.575-578). Examples such as *someone loves everyone, unfortunately* belongs to clause-oriented adjunct category. In this kind of examples, end positions for adverbs are strongly disfavoured unless there is a prosodic detachment. Our example in the paper is a kind of VP-oriented adjuncts and it prefers end position where prosodic detachment is not normal. Taken this grammatical note into account, we can stress that our example is correct without the need to use a comma before the adverb *expertly*.

wrongly by Morrill's complexity profiling. This objection which shows that Morrill's criteria are context sensitive would naturally lead us to demand a new proposal for multiple-quantifier sentences.

3 A New Proposal

Although it is true that Morrill's proposal fails in some cases related to the scoped readings, it is also true that it works rather well for other syntactic phenomena. Considering this fact, our strategy is to keep Morrill's criteria unchanged for those phenomena that work well and add a new procedure just for evaluating the complexity of quantification. We will see how we can filter out the complexity which can be raised by quantifiers. Formally, given two syntactic structures S_1, S_2 for a given sentence, the complexity can be evaluated in the following way:

$$C(S_1) > C(S_2) \iff (a_1, b_1) > (a_2, b_2)$$

where a_1, a_2 are the results of Morrill's criteria on S_1 and S_2, and b_1 and b_2 are the results of our proposal regarding quantifier order measurement (given in section 3.2). Notice that we are using lexicographical order, namely, $(a_1, b_1) > (a_2, b_2)$ iff $(a_1 > a_2)$ or $(a_1 = a_2$ and $b_1 > b_2)$. Broadly speaking, we will take the following steps:

1. Using in situ quantifier type assignment for construction the categorial proof-nets in order to filter out the quantifier effects in complexity profiling phase. (Described in sub-section 3.1)
2. Measuring syntactic complexity profiles for the previous step.
3. Measuring quantifier distance for different valid readings. (Described in sub-section 3.2)
4. Introducing the preference relations from the last two steps.

3.1 In situ (=Overbinding) Quantification

Hilbert's ϵ-calculus (Hilbert (1922)) is receiving a renewed interest. In particular, the application of ϵ-calculus to linguistics is becoming appreciated[4]. Our strategy for neutralizing quantifier effects in our complexity measurement on syntactic proof-nets can take place by exploiting Hilbert's ϵ-calculus in our semantic recipes.

In Hilbert's epsilon aside from the usual terms of first order logic, we have the ϵ and τ terms. In particular if A is a formula and x is a variable then $\epsilon_x A$ $(\tau_x A)$ are terms where all the occurrences of x in A are bound by ϵ (τ). What is interesting about this terms is that they express existential and universal quantification. In particular, $\epsilon_x A$ is the generic existential element and $\tau_x A$ is the generic universal element. The proper type for ϵ and τ is $(e \to t) \to e$. If we want to translate the sentence *All man are brave*, using the τ-binder, we can rewrite it as $brave(\tau_x man(x))$. As we can see an ϵ expressions can take scope over the entire sentence even if its occurrence is nested in the parsed tree.

We can observe that the formula $ate(\epsilon\lambda y.(pizza\ y), \tau\lambda x.(child\ x))$ is a proper translation for the sentence *Every children ate a pizza* in Hilbert epsilon fashion. This formula does not correspond to any usual logical formula and it is very similar to underspecified representation. This underspecified representation which properly corresponds to syntax tree can help us to filter out the effect of quantifiers for the sentences in the complexity measurement phase of the categorial proof-nets. We do not have to perform the quantifier type raising in the syntactic phase in order to properly represent quantification. So, we can keep the syntactic type of quantifiers as being np/n. As discussed, typed Hilbert's epsilon

[4]For an introductory explanation on Hilbert epsilon see Chatzikyriakidis et al. (2017) and (Retoré, 2014, p.218-221).

(Retoré, 2014, p.218-221) suggests some properties that does not exists in other underspecified representations (Copestake et al. (2005), Cooper (1983) and Steedman (1999)). The first projection, namely a in our complexity pair representation (a, b), can be introduced by the following procedure:

1. Define np/n syntactic categories to all determiners and quantifiers in our lexicon.
2. Define proper Hilbert epsilon semantical representation for the quantifiers in our lexical recipes.
3. Construct the categorial proof-nets for the sentence with the categorial assignments in our lexicon and plug the lexical recipes to each word.
4. Calculate the complexity measurement profiles of all the valid constructed categorial proof-nets gained in the previous step. This is the first projection of the pairs in our preference semantic model.

3.2 Quantifiers Order Measurement

Now, we can introduce the second projection, namely b, in our complexity pair representation (a, b):

1. Given the logical formula which corresponds to the left-to-right reading of the sentence; add an index from 1 to n to each quantifier from left to right obtaining $Q_1, Q_2 \ldots, Q_{n-1}, Q_n F$ call this formula Φ.
2. By the procedure introduced in (Hobbs and Shieber, 1987, p.49-53), derive all the valid quantifier (scope) readings of the sentence.
3. Let $\xi_1, \ldots, \xi_m$ be rewritten formulas obtained from the previous step.
4. Calculate for each ξ_i the penalty of quantifiers re-ordering as $\dfrac{1}{\sum_{j=1}^{n} \mid j - Pos(Q_j, \xi_i) \mid +1}$ in which $Pos(Q_j, \xi_i)$ is the occurrence position of the quantifier Q_j in ξ_i counted from left to right and incremented from number one.
5. The preference measurement on the quantifier ordering of each valid logical readings is gained from applying the previous step to all $\xi_1, \ldots, \xi_m$.

Figure 2: New Procedure for Example (1)

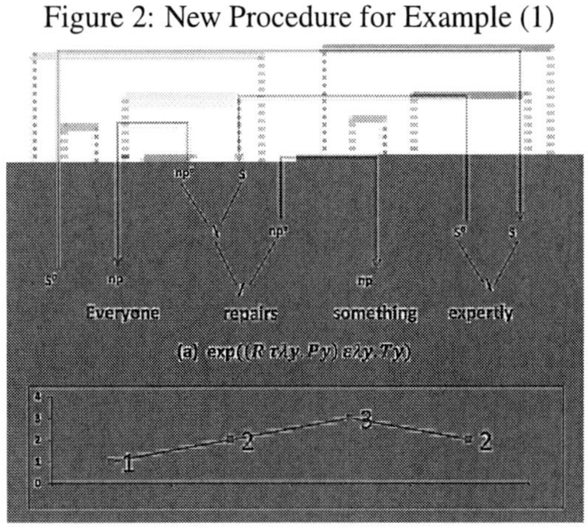

Let us re-calculate the complexity profile of the example (1) with our new proposal. By the procedure provided in (3.1) we can have the proof-net as it is shown in the figure (2). By assigning the semantic recipes and having the associated λ-term to the proof-net we will have the unspecified semantic representation that naturally corresponds to the linguistic syntactic structure[5]. As the effect of quantifiers is neutralized we can see that the first projection of our pair is fixed by the number 8. So, we can calculate the second projection namely the score for each reading using the procedure in (3.2), thus we have:

Reading (a) is $\frac{1}{(|1-1|+|2-2|)+1} = 1$, and reading (b) is $\frac{1}{(|1-2|+|2-1|)+1} = \frac{1}{3}$
Thus, we have $(8, 1) > (8, 0.3)$, and this shows that reading (a) is preferred to reading (b). All in all, the new proposal truly predicts the quantifier left-to-right scoping while the Morrill's criteria did not.

4 Conclusion and Possible Extensions

We have reported an issue provided by some counter examples on Morrill's complexity profiling approach. We showed how exploiting Hilbert epsilon can neutralize the quantifier effect and let us introduce a new procedure for measuring the complexity of quantifier scoping. We can extend our on-going project in the following directions: (i) ideally, there should be a dataset annotated for human-preferred readings of various naturally occurring utterances. In the absence of this, we are going to create a test suite illustrating the various phenomena that interact with quantifier scope preferences, and then to evaluate and extend it with the proposed method over that test-suite. This experiment would pave the way to the extension of our model by integrating other aspects such as common-sense knowledge and lexical semantics. (ii) we can exploit Montagovian Generative Lexicon framework (Retoré (2014)) that uses multi-sorted logical formulas. This choice would let us apply semantic distance approaches (Nagao (1994)) by using lexico-semantic networks such as Jeux-De-Mot (Lafourcade (2007); Chatzikyriakidis et al. (2015)).

5 Acknowledgement

We would like to express our gratitude to Christian Retoré and Richard Moot for their great support and constructive discussion during this research. We would also like to thank Jean-Philippe Prost and three anonymous reviewers for their insightful comments.

References

Chatzikyriakidis, S., M. Lafourcade, L. Ramadier, and M. Zarrouk (2015). Type theories and lexical networks: Using serious games as the basis for multi-sorted typed systems. In *ESSLLI: European Summer School in Logic, Language and Information.*

Chatzikyriakidis, S., F. Pasquali, and C. Retoré (2017). From logical and linguistic generics to hilberts tau and epsilon quantifiers. *IfCoLog Journal of Logics and their Applications 4*(2), 231–255.

Cooper, R. (1983). Quantification and syntactic theory, reidel, dordrecht. *CooperQuantification and Syntactic Theory1983.*

[5]An anonymous reviewer has pointed out an objection: our proposed epsilon-style representation is not generally valid because of the equivalence $\tau_x Px \equiv \epsilon x \neg Px$, and the fact that the epsilon is intuitively interpreted as a choice function. This will affect us when non-P ($\neg P$) is chosen by the choice function. This objection will not cause any problem for our proposal since, firstly, the equivalence is not valid in intuitionistic logic; secondly, even if we use classical epsilon-calculus, it is debatable that $\epsilon - terms$ can be interpreted as choice functions. In fact, choice functions are only defined on non-empty domains. If we consider a domain of interpretation, where each element is in P, we can not interpret ϵ as a choice function given that there is no non-empty subset of $\neg P$ where the choice function can be defined. To our knowledge, there is no completely satisfactory model of the epsilon-calculus aside from the indexed version as in Leiß (2017).

Copestake, A., D. Flickinger, C. Pollard, and I. A. Sag (2005). Minimal recursion semantics: An introduction. *Research on Language and Computation 3*(2-3), 281–332.

Durand-Guerrier, V. (2016). Négation et quantification dans la classe de mathématiques.

Hilbert, D. (1922). Die logischen grundlagen der mathematik. *Mathematische Annalen 88*(1), 151–165.

Hobbs, J. R. and S. M. Shieber (1987). An algorithm for generating quantifier scopings. *Computational Linguistics 13*(1-2), 47–63.

Huddleston, R., G. K. Pullum, et al. (2002). The cambridge grammar of english. *Language. Cambridge: Cambridge University Press*, 1–23.

Johnson, M. (1998). Proof nets and the complexity of processing center embedded constructions. *Journal of Logic, Language and Information 7*(4), 433–447.

Keller, W. R. (1988). Nested cooper storage: The proper treatment of quantification in ordinary noun phrases. In *Natural language parsing and linguistic theories*, pp. 432–447. Springer.

Lafourcade, M. (2007). Making people play for Lexical Acquisition with the JeuxDeMots prototype. In *7th International Symposium on Natural Language Processing (SNLP'07)*.

Lambek, J. (1958). The mathematics of sentence structure. *The American Mathematical Monthly 65*(3), 154–170.

Leiß, H. (2017). On equality of contexts and completeness of the indexed epsilon-calculus. *IfCoLog Journal of Logics and their Applications 4*(2), 347–366.

Moot, R. (2012). Wide-coverage semantics for spatio-temporal reasoning. *Traitement Automatique des Languages 53*(2), 115–142.

Moot, R. (2017). The Grail theorem prover: Type theory for syntax and semantics. In Z. Luo and S. Chatzikyriakidis (Eds.), *Modern Perspectives in Type Theoretical Semantics*. Springer. to appear.

Moot, R. and C. Retoré (2012). *The logic of categorial grammars: a deductive account of natural language syntax and semantics*, Volume 6850. Springer.

Morrill, G. (2000). Incremental processing and acceptability. *Computational linguistics 26*(3), 319–338.

Nagao, K. (1994). A preferential constraint satisfaction technique for natural language analysis. *IEICE TRANSACTIONS on Information and Systems 77*(2), 161–170.

Retoré, C. (2014). The montagovian generative lexicon lambda tyn: a type theoretical framework for natural language semantics. In *19th international conference on types for proofs and programs (TYPES 2013)*, Volume 26, pp. 202–229.

Steedman, M. (1999). Alternating quantifier scope in ccg. In *Proceedings of the 37th annual meeting of the Association for Computational Linguistics on Computational Linguistics*, pp. 301–308. Association for Computational Linguistics.

Steedman, M. (2012). *Taking scope: The natural semantics of quantifiers*. MIT Press.

An overview of Natural Language Inference Data Collection: The way forward?

Stergios Chatzikyriakidis, Robin Cooper, Simon Dobnik, Staffan Larsson
Centre for Linguistic Theory and Studies in Probability (CLASP)
Dept. of Philosophy, Linguistics and Theory of Science
University of Gothenburg
stergios.chatzikyriakidis@gu.se, cooper@ling.gu.se,
simon.dobnik@gu.se, sl@ling.gu.se

1 Introduction

Understanding a Natural Language (NL) sentence amounts to understanding its consequences as well as the sentences that it is a consequence of. As Cooper et al. (1996) aptly put it 'inferential ability is not only a central manifestation of semantic competence but is in fact centrally constitutive of it' . Given the latter claim, it is no surprise that the same authors argue that the best way to test the semantic adequacy of NLP systems is to look at how well they perform with regard to Natural Language Inference (NLI). It is very hard not to agree with this statement. Indeed, NLI is considered by many researchers to be the crux of computational semantics. This paper is about the datasets created for this need. In particular, we discuss the most common NLI resources arguing that all these a) fail to capture the wealth of inferential mechanisms present in NLI and b) seem to be driven by the dominant discourse in the field at the time of their creation. In light of these observations, we want to discuss the requirements that an adequate NLI platform must satisfy both in terms of the range of inference patterns found in reasoning with NL as well as the range of the data collection mechanisms that are needed in order to acquire this range of inferential patterns.

2 NLI datasets

In this section we present the merits and drawbacks of three NLI datasets which represent some of the main strategies that have been used in the data collection of inference.

2.1 The FraCaS test suite

The FraCaS test suite was built in the mid 1990's by the FraCaS project, an EU project aimed at developing a general framework for computational semantics (Cooper et al., 1996).[1] It was later recast in machine-readable form by Bill McCartney of Stanford University.[2] The data set consists of 346 problems each containing one or more statements and one yes/no-question (except for four problems, where there is no question). The total number of sentences in the data set is 1220, but since some of them are repeated in several problems, there are in total 874 unique sentences.

The FraCaS test suite has been later extended into the MultiFraCaS, which includes a translation of the test suite into German, Farsi, Mandarin and Greek.[3] There is also the Japanese FraCaS extension (JSem), which expands the original FraCaS after translation in a number of ways: it contains basic patterns of semantic inferences such as active-passive alternation and adverbial phrases not included in

[1] ftp://ftp.cogsci.ed.ac.uk/pub/FRACAS/del16.ps.gz
[2] www-nlp.stanford.edu/~wcmac/downloads/fracas.xml
[3] www.ling.gu.se/~cooper/multifracas/.

the original FraCaS and further extends the original set with constructions specific to Japanese syntax and semantics that have been discussed in the literature. Furthermore, the types of inferences are annotated.[4]

Merits: even though it contains only 346 examples, it covers a lot of inference cases and it now has the advantage of some multilinguality

Drawbacks: the examples are mostly logical inferences, the data are constructed and the dataset is very small especially with today's standards.

2.2 Recognizing Textual Entailment

The Recognizing Textual Entailment (RTE) challenges were first developed in 2004 as a means to test textual entailment, i.e. relations between a premise text and a hypothesis text. RTE uses naturally occurring data as premises and then constructs the hypothesis text based on the premise natural text. The first RTE challenge makes a binary classification of entailment, i.e. a hypothesis is either entailed or non-entailed. This is changed to a tripartite classification (hypothesis entailed, its negation entailed or no entailment) in RTE4 and RTE5 (Giampiccolo et al., 2008; Bentivogli et al., 2009).

Merits The RTE challenges remedy the unnaturalness of constructed examples by using examples from natural text and furthermore make a first step of including entailments that require presupposed information, including non-logical presuppositional inferences.

Drawbacks Even though the RTE platforms have been notoriously difficult for NLI systems (especially the three way entailment tasks), most of the examples do not involve deep semantic inference but are rather complicated in terms of their syntax. Furthermore, the definition of inference assumed in a number of the examples is problematic. As Zaenen et al. (2005) have pointed out, RTE platforms suffer from cases of inference that should not be categorised as such. For these cases, a vast amount of world knowledge needs to be taken into consideration (that most importantly not every linguistic agent has). The problem is that there is no clear annotation that will distinguish different kinds of inference. Lastly, and similarly to the FraCaS, the RTE datasets are still very small (less than 1000 pairs for both the development and the test set for all challenges) compared with approaches that rely on large datasets such as Deep Learning approaches (DL).

2.3 Stanford Natural Language Inference

A recent data collection for NLI was developed in Stanford by Bowman et al. (2015) using crowdsourcing (Mechanical Turk). The subjects are given a caption of a picture and are then asked to provide: a) an alternate true caption b) an alternate possibly true caption and c) an alternate false caption. The dataset constructed out of this process contains 570k inference pairs, making SNLI two orders of magnitude bigger than the previous datasets.

Merits The size of the corpus makes it suitable for training DL approaches. The SNLI platform is an extremely useful resource, and given the current state of affairs in computational linguistics, it is the only one that is usable for approaches using DL, which are predominant at the moment. Furthermore, reasoning in SNLI is tied to specific situations.

[4]We thank an anonymous reviewer for this information as regards the Japanese FraCaS. More info can be found here: `http://researchmap.jp/community-inf/JSeM/?lang=english`. Also for a discussion on JSem please consult Kawazoe et al. (2015).

Drawbacks Situational reasoning can be also claimed to be a drawback of SNLI. What would be for example the image described by a caption "all men are human"? It appears that quantification requires evaluation of collections of image/description pairs. Furthermore, and similarly to earlier platforms, SNLI seems to capture only a fraction of the range of phenomena associated with NLI.

2.4 Some other NLI platforms

There exist a number of lesser known, theory specific or, at a first sight not NLI related datasets used for NLI. We mention briefly three here:

- the SICK dataset (Sentences Involving Compositional Knowledge) (Marelli et al., 2014) is a dataset created to test compositional distributional semantics (DS) models. Although the dataset contains examples that one would count as belonging to logical inference (negation, conjunction, disjunction, apposition, relative clauses, etc.), its focus are distributional semantic approaches and therefore it normalises several cases DS is not expected to account for. For example, named entities are turned into noun phrases standing for the class, and complex VPs and sentences involving modals and auxiliaries are simplified.[5]
- The PPDB (Paraphrase Database) relation extraction dataset (Ganitkevitch et al., 2015) is primarily a dataset on paraphrase. However, it is further annotated for entailment (unidirectional, bidirectional etc.), making it extremely useful for entailment tasks as well.
- The VQA (Visual Question Answering) corpus[6] contains open-ended questions (and answers) about images. While SNLI models inference from linguistic and perceptual data together, one could see the VQA task as inference from perceptual input alone, but guided by linguistic input (the question). The output in both cases are NL sentences[7]. We believe that inference from perceptual input should be included when constructing a state-of-the-art NLI dataset.

3 The way forward

3.1 What do we need?

We need to include more kinds of inference than were originally in the FraCaS test suite. In addition to classical logical inference we further need presuppositional inference and non-logical inference as given by implicatures and enthymemes[8]. Presuppositional inference is to some extent included implicitly in the FraCaS test suite but it is treated as logical inference implicitly.[9]

We also need to include examples of probabilistic reasoning relating to conditional probability though we need to be clear with this whether we are referring to probabilistic judgements made by individuals

[5] Given the fact that the SICK dataset involves a lot of cases one would classify as logical inference, it is not surprising to find systems based on logic being evaluated on this dataset, Abzianidze (2015); Martınez-Gómez et al. (2017).

[6] `http://www.visualqa.org/`

[7] For VQA, given an y/n-question $P?$, answer "yes" means inference is P and "no" means inference is $\neg P$, and given a wh-question $?x.p(x)$, the answer a means the inference is $p(a)$.

[8] An enthymeme is a logic-like deductive inference with one or several premises supplied by context (Breitholtz and Villing, 2008). For example, in a discussion about which road to take, the premise "Walnut Street is shorter" may lead to the conclusion "We should take Walnut Street", assuming a hidden premise "If X is the shortest route, we should take X".

[9] For example, section 9 in the FraCaS test suite involves presuppositional rather than logical inference:

P1 Smith knew that ITEL had won the contract in 1992.

Q Did ITEL win the contract in 1992?

H ITEL won the contract in 1992. [FraCaS 334]

A more fine-grained platform for NLI would have recognised this fact and would also include a case where complement presupposition survives under negation by changing P1 into *Smith did not know that ITEL had won the contract in 1992.*

or probabilities that individual agents will make the corresponding categorical judgement. It would be an advantage to have data of both kinds.[10]

It is important that the data set be grounded in real data so that it does not just represent armchair intuitions of linguistic experts as the FraCaS test suite does. It also seems important to us that the real data should include reasoning in interactive dialogue settings and not just text (as, for example, in the textual entailment enterprise). Furthermore, there has been a significant interest in connecting language and vision recently and exploring inference in this context appears to be a promising and challenging research field. For example, Marconi (1997) distinguishes between inferential meanings of words, which enables inferences from uses of the word, and referential meaning, allowing speakers to identify the objects and situations referred to by the word.[11] A key property to explore here is how different modalities provide information for an acceptable inference. For example "A group of children enjoy their time on the beach" and "A group of adults are swimming at the beach"[12] can be considered a contradiction, provided that there exists sufficient visual information supporting this.

3.2 How to get it?

The emphasis on real data does not necessarily mean that we should abandon constructed examples as one form of input, but it does mean that constructed examples should be grounded in real data either by (i) finding corresponding examples in corpora consisting of text from different genres or the web; and (ii) by conducting experiments in which subjects are asked to evaluate or construct inferences using both textual and visual context. In the latter case we think it is useful (iii) to use crowd-sourcing and (iv) to adapt the game techniques used in GWAPs (Games with a Purpose), for example in a way they were used for construction of lexico-semantic networks (Lafourcade, 2011)[13].

3.3 How we know we got it?

In order to address the issue of verifying of NLI datasets constructed by expert semanticists in the intuitions of speakers of a language we conducted a pilot study based on the inference examples from the FraCaS suite (Cooper et al., 1996). The purpose of this evaluation is two-fold: (i) to verify whether intuitions of inference of ordinary speakers correspond to the intuitions of the authors of the dataset; and (ii) to evaluate a degree of variation of inference intuitions for individual examples which would allow us to examine how humans reason and therefore further study examples of inference that are normally considered as problematic. We selected 15 "interesting" examples (those that in our experience are either very clear in terms of the inference label and those that are problematic) covering quantification (2, 6, 12, 17, 38, 74), adjectives (199, 201, 206, 211, 212, 223), and other semantic phenomena including plurals (103), sluicing (163), and temporal reference (308). The examples were chosen so that there were 5 examples of each inference class *yes*, *no*, and *don't know+undefined*, using the labels from (MacCartney, 2007). The task was framed as a controlled crowd-sourcing data collection experiment using the Semant-o-matic tool[14], previously used to collect data in related tasks such as (Dobnik et al., 2014; Dobnik and Åstbom, 2017). In contrast to other crowd-sourcing solutions, a specialised tool allows us to target particular groups of individuals through social media and therefore combines the properties of controlled data-collection experiments with online crowd-sourcing. Examples of inference were presented

[10] It is worth repeating here that annotation for different types of inferences (not including probabilistic inference) has been done for the Japanese extension of the FraCaS, JSem, Kawazoe et al. (2015). In connection to probabilistic inference, it would be interesting to have a look at STS (Semantic Textual Similarity) datasets. These present a similarity score (ranging from 1 to 5), which can potentially be seen as a probabilistic judgement. Such scores are also present in the SICK dataset. It might be worth looking at the way these similarity scores reflect in some way the type of probabilistic inference we are discussing here.

[11] While SNLI models inference from linguistic and hypothetical perceptual scenarios together, one could see the VQA task as inference from perceptual input alone, but guided by linguistic input (the question).

[12] Example from SNLI provided by a reviewer.

[13] `www.jeuxdemots.org`

[14] `http://www.dobnik.net/simon/semant-o-matic/`

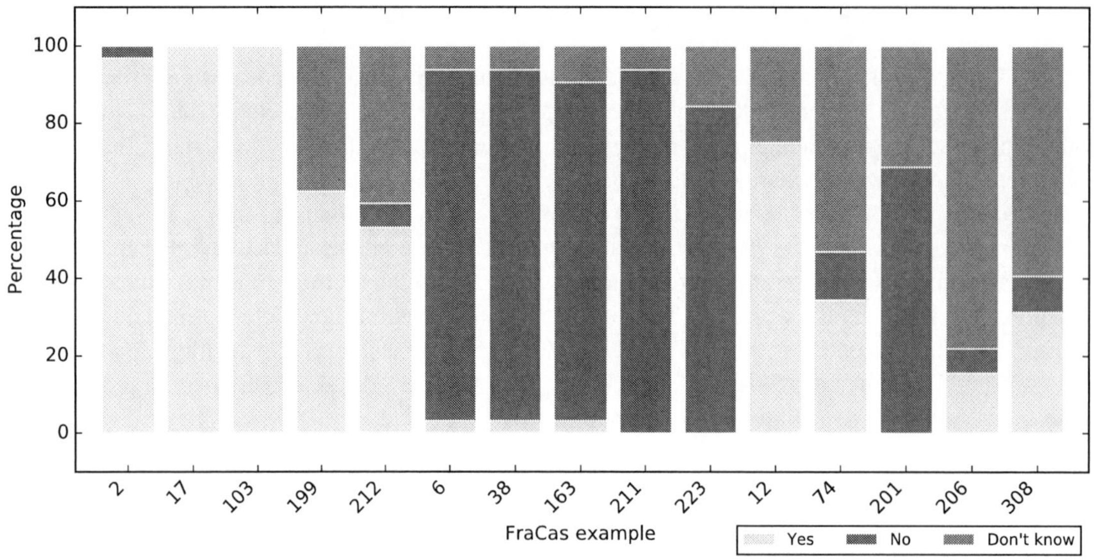

Figure 1: Judgements of 46 participants for four inference labels in FraCaS 'yes' (2, 17, 103, 199, 212), 'no' (6, 38, 163, 211, 223) and 'don't know' (74, 201, 206) + 'undefined' (12, 308).

as one or more statements (representing premises) and a question corresponding to the conclusion. Participants were instructed to answer the question choosing one of the three categories (yes, no and don't know) by only considering information contained in the sentences. Note that our answer *don't know* is different from the *don't know* category in FraCaS as it also includes cases that FraCaS labels as *undefined*. Hence, our category capture all cases where one cannot provide a *yes* and *no* answer from the information contained in the sentences but with some additional knowledge this would be possible.[15]

We recruited 46 participants, mostly employees (academic and non-academic) at University of Gothenburg some of whom are native speakers of English but the majority of participants had Swedish as their first language with excellent command of English. The results of their judgements are shown in Figure 1. Overall there is a strong agreement with the FraCas score on *yes* and *no* classes. Sometimes examples of the *yes* and *no* classes are labelled as *don't know*. Most variation exists in the *don't know* class, where some participants are likely to answer *yes*, possibly because they are bringing in additional background knowledge which allows them to draw a conclusion. The results also point out to examples within the FraCaS suite where the choice of the label may not be straightforward. For example, both 199 and 201 involve interpretation of adjectival scope ("former successful university student"). Results also indicate that the label *don't know* may also be assigned in cases where there are several premises and relations between premises which are likely contribute to high cognitive load and participants simply give up making an inference (example 212). We are extending the evaluation of the FraCas in our ongoing and future work by including (i) more examples; (ii) more participants; (ii) participants with different backgrounds (students who attended a computational semantics class vs non-experts); and (iii) different languages (currently Slovenian and Greek). Figure 1 may be given probabilistic interpretation as internalised beliefs of an agent about the most likely conclusion to draw after observing drawing of conclusions of other agents (Cooper et al., 2015). An alternative probabilistic model of inference is to query individual participants directly to indicate their degree of belief (rather than using 3 categories used in FraCaS) that an inference holds using a gradient scale with a help of an unlabelled slider (as in Dobnik and Åstbom, 2017) which we intend to explore in our future work.

[15]The task can be accessed at `https://linux.dobnik.net/simon/experiments/semant-o-matic/interface.en.flov.php?conversation=presentation_test`.

References

Abzianidze, L. (2015). A tableau prover for natural logic and language. In *Proceedings of EMNLP15.*

Bentivogli, L., P. Clark, I. Dagan, and D. Giampiccolo (2009). The fifth PASCAL recognizing textual entailment challenge. In *TAC.*

Bowman, S. R., G. Angeli, C. Potts, and C. D. Manning (2015). A large annotated corpus for learning natural language inference. In *Proceedings of EMNLP*, pp. 632–642.

Breitholtz, E. and J. Villing (2008). Can aristotelian enthymemes decrease the cognitive load of a dialogue system user. In *Proceedings of the 12th Workshop on the Semantics and Pragmatics of Dialogue (SemDial 2008, 'LonDial')*, pp. 94–100.

Cooper, R., D. Crouch, J. van Eijck, C. Fox, J. van Genabith, J. Jaspars, H. Kamp, D. Milward, M. Pinkal, M. Poesio, and S. Pulman (1996). Using the framework. Technical report LRE 62-051r, The FraCaS consortium. `ftp://ftp.cogsci.ed.ac.uk/pub/FRACAS/del16.ps.gz`.

Cooper, R., S. Dobnik, S. Lappin, and S. Larsson (2015, November). Probabilistic type theory and natural language semantics. *Linguistic Issues in Language Technology — LiLT 10*(4), 1–43.

Dobnik, S. and A. Åstbom (2017, August 15–17). (Perceptual) grounding as interaction. In V. Petukhova and Y. Tian (Eds.), *Proceedings of Saardial – Semdial 2017: The 21st Workshop on the Semantics and Pragmatics of Dialogue*, Saarbrücken, Germany, pp. 17–26.

Dobnik, S., J. D. Kelleher, and C. Koniaris (2014, 1–3 September). Priming and alignment of frame of reference in situated conversation. In V. Rieser and P. Muller (Eds.), *Proceedings of DialWatt – Semdial 2014: The 18th Workshop on the Semantics and Pragmatics of Dialogue*, Edinburgh, pp. 43–52.

Ganitkevitch, E., P. Pavlick, J. Rastogi, B. Van Durme, and C. Callison-Burch (2015, July 26–31). PPDB 2.0: Better paraphrase ranking, fine-grained entailment relations, word embeddings, and style classification. In *Proceedings of the 53rd Annual Meeting of the Association for Computational Linguistics and the 7th International Joint Conference on Natural Language Processing (Short Papers)*, Beijing, China, pp. 425–430. Association for Computational Linguistics.

Giampiccolo, D., H. T. Dang, B. Magnini, I. Dagan, E. Cabrio, and W. B. Dolan (2008). The fourth PASCAL recognizing textual entailment challenge. In *TAC.*

Kawazoe, A., R. Tanaka, K. Mineshima, and D. Bekki (2015). An inference problem set for evaluating semantic theories and semantic processing systems for Japanese. In *JSAI International Symposium on Artificial Intelligence*, pp. 58–65. Springer.

Lafourcade, M. (2011, December 8). *Lexique et analyse sémantique de textes - structures, acquisitions, calculs, et jeux de mots.* tel-00649851, Université Montpellier II - Sciences et Techniques du Languedoc.

MacCartney, B. (2007). The FraCaS textual inference problem set. Online resource, `http://www-nlp.stanford.edu/~wcmac/downloads/fracas.xml`, Stanford University.

Marconi, D. (1997). *Lexical competence.* Cambridge, Mass.: MIT Press.

Marelli, M., S. Menini, M. Baroni, L. Bentivogli, R. Bernardi, and R. Zamparelli (2014). A SICK cure for the evaluation of compositional distributional semantic models. In *LREC*, pp. 216–223.

Martınez-Gómez, P., K. Mineshima, Y. Miyao, and D. Bekki (2017). On-demand injection of lexical knowledge for recognising textual entailment. In *Proceedings of the 17th Conference of the European Chapter of the Association for Computational Linguistics (EACL'17).*

Zaenen, A., L. Karttunen, and R. Crouch (2005). Local textual inference: can it be defined or circumscribed? In *Proceedings of the ACL workshop on empirical modeling of semantic equivalence and entailment*, pp. 31–36. Association for Computational Linguistics.

Explicative Path Finding in a Semantic Network

Kévin Cousot, Mathieu Lafourcade
LIRMM / Campus St Priest, 161 Rue Ada, 34090 Montpellier, France
kevin.cousot@lirmm.fr, mathieu.lafourcade@lirmm.fr

Introduction

When building a knowledge base (KB), it is desirable to be able to assess its quality, and one approach to undertake such a task is to exhibit explanation(s) related to contained information. For example, from an information stating that (a) *tiger 'characteristic' dangerous*, we would like to be able to ask *Why ?* and obtaining at least one explanation, for example *tiger 'is-a' 'wild animal' characteristic' dangerous* or something more elaborated like *tiger 'agent' attack 'consequence' death & dangerous 'consequence' death.* These explanations take the form of *explicative* path in the KB, and can be good clues of the quality of the knowledge present in the database. To do so, the KB has to be represented (or converted) under the form of a lexico-semantic network (for instance, like Wordnet or Babelnet).

After presenting some related work, we detail some aspects of the JeuxDeMots lexical network on which we undertook our modeling and experiment. Then, we introduce our method, the *explicative path finding by triangulation* and some evaluation.

1 Related work

Path finding in semantic resources is used in several applications. Path finding has been used in *information retrieval* to improve ranking over semantic web resources and results relevance (Lee et al., 2009). In that work, paths are explored in an ontology from user query keywords and available resources. Every path is not meaningful and, in order to limit processing useless paths only those matching some practical constraints are considered. Typically, for a path to be valid it is required that a relation's range is the same as the next relation's domain (or a subclass of it). Thus, paths look like : $writtenBy^{-1}(Prof, Publication) \wedge hasTitle(Publication, Str)$. The notation with the R^{-1} is R with the order of its arguments inverted. Once meaningful paths are found, they are then weighted according to the information content of their relations and mutual information of the entities they link. With those metrics it is possible to order paths according to their relevance. Path length is taken into account by decreasing the path weight as length increases because shorter paths are assumed to be more relevant. Finally, retrieved resources are ranked according to the number of meaningful paths, keyword coverage and their distinguishability.

In *text-mining*, (Song et al., 2015) use semantic paths to explore large text corpora and try to find relations between entities such as treatments and secondary effects. To perform closed-discovery, two terms are given to the system, source and target, which tries to infer intermediate terms between them. Intermediate, or linking terms are obtained from text corpora using text mining techniques. In particular, entities are extracted using a NER software and mapped to Unified Medical Language System (UMLS) while relations come directly from biomedical verbs identified in the corpora. The same process is applied to the linked terms, building a graph step after step. The graph's edges are weighted according to several similarity measures such as Path (Lin, 1998) and LCH (Leacock and Chodorow, 1998). Eventually, found paths are evaluated by experts (people in NLP) and native speakers.

Some research focused on causality. In (Besnard et al., 2008) an inference system able to provide explanations of causal statements is developed. Based on first order logic, it introduces a language to express causal statements (such as *On(alarm) causes Heard(bell)*) and truths (*Heard(soft_bell)* $\Longrightarrow$ $\neg$ *Heard(loud_bell)*). In this language, predicates are unary and express facts related to entities whereas constants are elements of an ontology listing (entities and their is-a relationships). From this, causal (α causes β) and explanation (α explains β because ϕ) atoms are introduced. A set of patterns manually defined then make it possible to infer explanations by exploiting the ontology (which allows generalization : if b is-a a then $p(b)$ entails $p(a)$) and explanation transitivity.

2 RezoJDM : the JeuxDeMots lexical-semantic network

JeuxDeMots (Lafourcade, 2007) is a construction environment for RezoJDM, a lexical-semantic network for French. It is a graph whose vertices are labeled with terms, concepts or any kind of text expression. Edges are oriented, weighted and typed with either lexical (lemma, location, action to verb, ...) or semantic (hypernymy, meronymy, agent, ...) relations. Over 100 different lexical and semantic types are available. In the following, we use indistinctly the terms *edge* and *relation*. In particular, polysemy, or some more precise usage of a word is expressed through the semantic refinement (*raff_sem*) relation type. For example, the word *avocat* has two meanings : it is either referring to *lawyer* (*juriste*) or *avocado* (*fruit*). This knowledge is encoded in the network with 3 vertices and 2 edges :

$$avocat \xrightarrow{raff\_sem} avocat{>}juriste$$
$$avocat \xrightarrow{raff\_sem} avocat{>}fruit$$

The weight of the relation expresses the strength o f association with the following principle : the higher the weight, the more relevant the relation between the terms (relatively to other relations with lower weight). Impossibilities and exceptions are identified with a negative weight. Typically : *fly* $\xrightarrow{\text{agent/-100}}$ *ostrich*. The weights are the result of the player activity in the JeuxDeMots games, i. e. the more a term is associated by player the highest the relation weight. Labelled vertices can also be linked to miscellaneous informations such as their polarity (positive, negative, neutral), some conceptual information, their color if any, or even a political connotation.

RezoJDM is built by combining different inputs. For the most part, data is collected via GWAPs[1] in which players participate to the network expansion by providing new terms and relations or consolidating them. Direct contributions can be done through Diko[2] a collaborative dictionary that allows users to edit the network and add, validate or correct knowledge data. Different inference mechanisms also continuously explore the network, generating new data (Zarrouk et al., 2013). So far, RezoJDM has more than 1.5 millions vertices and 100 millions relations.

3 Explicative path finding by triangulation

RezoJDM is a small world network : the diameter is quite small (around 6) as terms are often linked to hubs (terms with a large number of edges, such as *animal*, *person*, *place*, *process*, etc. The weights of relations are distributed according a power law. Theses properties are very interesting as it makes many exploration heuristics possible and as such a lot of raw facts are easily accessible through high-level knowledge. For example, the following fact is correct :

$$drug \xrightarrow{against} disease$$

But this is not self-explanatory and it does not tell us very well why drugs are acting against diseases.. We believe more information would be inferred by focusing on paths instead on direct relations :

$$drug \xrightarrow{instr^{-1}} healing \xrightarrow{against} disease$$

The interest of an explicative path is to provide such an explanation, which gives clues of the rightfulness of the KB. Wrong paths can pinpoint defects in the KB.

3.1 Our Approach

The inference of explanatory paths is based on **triangulation** : it is a matter of completing triangular relations arrangements by using the KB to find the relationship (s) that are lacking for the triangle to be complete.

1. Game With A Purpose
2. http ://www.jeuxdemots.org/diko.php

Starting from a true fact $x \xrightarrow{t} y$, **induction** consists in finding an intermediary vertex v connecting x and y. In order to maintain consistency, the (v, y) edge must have the same relation type t as the starting fact while (x, v) can be of any type. Not considering this constraint definitively leads to an increased number of nonsensical inferences. The result is an explicative path of length 2 (Figure 1).

For instance, to explain why *tiger* $\xrightarrow{carac}$ *dangerous*). we would like to get *tiger* $\xrightarrow{is\text{-}a}$ *wild animal* $\xrightarrow{carac}$ *dangerous*.

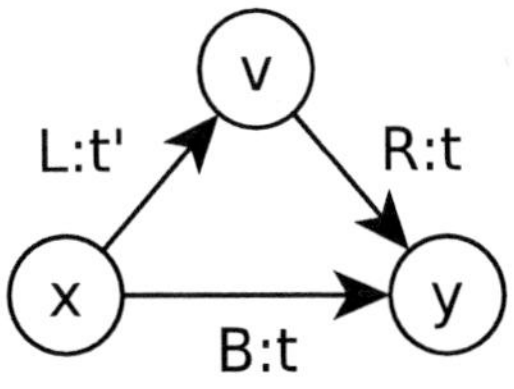

FIGURE 1 – Triangle schema with L(eft), (R)ight and B(ase) relations. Induction proposes possible pairs (LR) of relations t and t' from the initial (B) relation t. Conversely, consolidation proposes a possible initial relation (B) from a pair (LR).

The process is then applied recursively to the path's edges, expanding it and refining the explanation.

Beside the *triangulation*, there is dual operation named **consolidation**, which aims at finding in the KB a shortcut between two connected edges. In (Figure 1) finding a relation t from x, y is a consolidation. The consolidation task is undertaken along with induction.

The intermediary vertex choice is critical and one must choose a path that provides useful information. To tackle this task we use the confidence index from the data mining domain. Given two events X and Y, the confidence in the rule $X \rightarrow Y$ (X gives Y) is the quotient of X and Y joint probability and the probability of X :

$$conf(X \Rightarrow Y) = \frac{P(X,Y)}{P(X)} = \frac{P(RB)}{P(L)}$$

In our case, X is the number of occurrences of the following triangle's pattern (right hand side and base, RB) : $x \xrightarrow{t} y \xleftarrow{t} v$, while Y is the triangle's left hand side (L) : $x \xrightarrow{t'} v$. When co-occurring, X and Y form the triangle. Because only relation types (and not vertices) are relevant, we write $conf(t, t')$. For example, if the network contains 131 810 RB typed *agent* and 24 005 triangles with *instr* types for L then $conf(agent, instr) = 0.182$. At each step, the 3 vertices with the highest confidence are chosen. We also add an arbitrary threshold under which vertices are ignored. Other measures could have been considered such as activation distance (Lafourcade, 2011) or Pointwise Mutual Information (Bouma, 2009).

One question arises as why not is the confidence $conf(X \Rightarrow Y)$ defined as $\frac{P(RLB)}{P(B)}$ (instead of $\frac{P(RB)}{P(L)}$)? This comes from the two constraints we put on ourselves : first, we want triangles, second, B and R must be of same type. Therefore the confidence measure must allow us to chose the best amongst all possible L of type t'.

The confidence measure allows us to choose some intermediary vertices, nevertheless we also need a way to limit the graph's exploration. It is indeed pointless to continue the path's expansion to exhaustion (and certainly not computationally sound). As the path gets longer, it becomes more likely that it will contain irrelevant informations, we therefore limit its length. Likewise we limit the distance between the intermediary vertex and the starting fact vertices by using Jaccard index (Jaccard, 1901) :

$$J(x, y) = \frac{|\Gamma(x) \cap \Gamma(y)|}{|\Gamma(x) \cup \Gamma(y)|}$$

with x and y being two vertices and Γ the neighbor function which is the proportion of common neighbors. If a given J value falls below a given threshold, the expansion is canceled.

4 Evaluation

For the evaluation, the following parameters were used. We used the following semantic relation types : *is-a, charac(teristic), (has-)parts, place, against, agent, patient, instrument, consequence, implication and raff_sem.* Explicative paths length is limited to 5. We also set the minimum J to 1/3 and the minimum confidence to 0.5. We undertook two experiments and the produced explicative paths have been manually evaluated :

. On the medicine domain (M1) : 100 facts (related to this domain) have been randomly selected in the KB ;
. On general common sense (CS1) : 100 facts have been hand chosen (like *kettle* $\xrightarrow{agent}$ *burn*).

4.1 Results

Results are presented respectively in tables 1 and 2. Each path has been evaluated as valid, not valid or borderline (used when the evaluators have some difficulties evaluating the soundness of the path). Some acceptable path examples : *kettle* $\xrightarrow{place}$ *fire* $\xrightarrow{charac}$ *hot* $\xrightarrow{conseq}$ *burn*; and *avocado* $\xrightarrow{is\text{-}a}$ *fruit* $\xrightarrow{parts}$ *rind* $\xrightarrow{patient\text{-}of}$ *peel*;
Some borderline paths : *avocat* $\xrightarrow{is\text{-}a}$ *homme* $\xrightarrow{parts}$ *peau* $\xrightarrow{patient\text{-}of}$ *peler*; (Eng. *avocado/lawyer* $\xrightarrow{is\text{-}a}$ *man* $\xrightarrow{parts}$ *skin* $\xrightarrow{patient\text{-}of}$ *to peal*;) (as stated before, *avocat* and has two meanings : *lawyer* and *avocado*).

l	nb	valid	not valid	borderline
1	130	89	5	6
2	259	87	6	7
3	345	80	9	11
4	307	76	12	12
5	167	69	16	15

TABLE 1 – M1 results in % according to length of path (l). nb is the number of paths.

l	nb	valid	not valid	borderline
1	176	83	7	10
2	312	79	10	11
3	406	74	12	14
4	367	73	12	15
5	216	67	16	17

TABLE 2 – CS1 results in % according to length of path (l). nb is the number of paths.

The agreement between validators was fairly high, around 0.78 (the percentage of the common evaluation). They were arguing mostly on borderline paths which acceptability might vary accordingly with the validator. There was up to 5 validators and they were able to discuss their choice remotely through chat systems (Skype, Hangout, etc.). Validators were people involved somehow in the JeuxDeMots project and all of them have university degrees.

4.2 Discussion

First, we can compare the results for both experiments. CS1 seems more productive (as regards the number of paths) : from the same number of initial facts (100), CS1 systematically produces more path than M1. We should keep in mind than the number of paths in Table 1 and 1 does not represent all possible paths but only those selected by our method.

The method does not produce as good results on CS1 than M1, as there is always a higher percentage of invalid or borderline paths. A beginning of explanation might be that the common language is certainly more polysemous and vague than that of a specific domain like medicine. Another possible reason would be the judgment of the evaluators. They are certainly stricter in the general domain (common sens) which is often more meaningful for them than a specific domain.

In both experiments, the number of paths produced increases with length up to 3, then decreases. The negative impact of length tends to strongly filter the number of paths, hence there is not a combinatorial explosion of paths.

Conclusion

In this article we have presented an approach for computing explicative paths in a lexical-semantic network. We undertook some experiments through the JeuxDeMots network. The preliminary results we detailed are quite encouraging as they effectively allowed to assess the network quality and consolidate many knowledge tidbits.

As future work, we aim at comparing and combining path and to do such some similarity functions should be defined on paths of different length. Furthermore, identifying almost complete paths seems to be a good direction for a new type of inference, where some extended context could be taken into account.

References

Besnard, P., M.-O. Cordier, and Y. Moinard (2008). Ontology-based inference for causal explanation.

Bouma, G. (2009). Normalized (pointwise) mutual information in collocation extraction. *Proceedings of GSCL.*

Jaccard, P. (1901). *Etude comparative de la distribution florale dans une portion des Alpes et du Jura.* Impr. Corbaz.

Lafourcade, M. (2007). Making people play for Lexical Acquisition with the JeuxDeMots prototype. In *7th International Symposium on Natural Language Processing (SNLP'07).*

Lafourcade, M. (2011). *Lexique et analyse sémantique de textes - structures, acquisitions, calculs, et jeux de mots.* Ph. D. thesis.

Leacock, C. and M. Chodorow (1998). Combining local context with WordNet similarity for word sense identification.

Lee, J., J. Min, and C. Chung (2009). An Effective Semantic Search Technique Using Ontology. In *Proceedings of the 18th International Conference on World Wide Web.*

Lin, D. (1998). An Information-Theoretic Definition of Similarity.

Song, M., G. E. Heo, and Y. Ding (2015). SemPathFinder : Semantic path analysis for discovering publicly unknown knowledge. *Journal of Informetrics.*

Zarrouk, M., M. Lafourcade, and A. Joubert (2013). Inference and Reconciliation in a Crowdsourced Lexical-Semantic Network. *Proceedings of the 14th International Conference on Intelligent Text Processing and Computational Linguistics (CICLing).*

Correcting Contradictions

Aikaterini-Lida Kalouli
University of Konstanz
aikaterini-lida.kalouli@uni-konstanz.de

Livy Real
University of São Paulo
livyreal@gmail.com

Valeria de Paiva
Nuance Communications
valeria.depaiva@gmail.com

Abstract

This paper describes a manual investigation of the contradiction asymmetries of the SICK corpus, which is the intended testing set for a new system for natural language inference. Any system providing conceptual semantics for sentences, so that entailment-contradiction-neutrality relations between sentences can be identified, needs a baseline test set. The investigation of this test set, a part of the SICK corpus, was necessary to check the quality of our testing data and to ensure that the set is logically valid. This checking showed us that the lack of a specific context or reference for the sentence pairs and the presence of indefinite determiners have made the task of annotating very hard, leading to those contradiction asymmetries. We propose a way of correcting these annotations, which solves some of the issues but also makes some compromises.

1 Motivation

This paper describes our continuing work to analyse and improve the SICK corpus of English sentences created by Marelli et al. (2014). We aim to use SICK as a golden corpus for our studies on inference detection. SICK (Sentences Involving Compositional Knowledge) provides a benchmark for compositional distributional semantic models. The corpus consists of sentence pairs that are rich in the lexical, syntactic and semantic phenomena that distributional semantics are expected to account for. However, the corpus is simplified in other aspects: there are no named entities, the tenses have been simplified to the progressive only, there are few modifiers, few complex verb expressions, etc[1].

The data set consists of 9840 English sentence pairs, generated from existing sets of captions of pictures. The authors of SICK selected a subset of the caption sources and applied a 3-step generation process to obtain their pairs. This data was then sent to Amazon Turkers who annotated them for semantic similarity and for inference relations, i.e. for entailment, contradiction and neutral stances. Since SICK was created from captions of pictures, it contains literal, non-abstract, common-sense concepts and is thus considered a simple corpus for inference.

Given its intended simplicity the SICK corpus is a good dataset to test a collection of approaches for obtaining deeper semantic representations and to test text entailment evaluation methods. While the corpus seems to have been mostly used, so far, for distributional comparisons (Bowman et al. (2015); Beltagy et al. (2015)), we decided to try a more logic-based approach. Thus, we started investigating the corpus to see on the one hand, what non-expert annotators consider entailment-contradiction-neutrality relations and on the other hand what kinds of inferences are included in such a simple corpus. This should give us an idea of where a logic based pipeline might fail because of the lack of encyclopedic knowledge or the lack of higher reasoning mechanisms that humans possess.

[1]These characteristics are indeed true. However, as with any corpus, there are some issues.

2 The Problem: Contradictions are symmetric

Looking into the data, however, we realized that the corpus construction and annotation process produced a very surprising result. Contradictions in logic are symmetric but the human annotators produced several cases where contradictions are asymmetric. Since each annotator annotated each pair only in one direction, the corpus ended up with 611 pairs where the first of the sentences is deemed contradictory to the second, but the second sentence is neutral or – in a few cases – even entails the other. Since we want a logically valid corpus, we first needed to correct such annotations that we deemed wrong and this led us to analyze the possible reasons for those mistakes.

In our previous work (Kalouli et al. (2017)), we manually looked at and corrected all 1513 pairs of one-sided entailments, notated in the corpus as $AeBBnA$ (meaning pairs where sentence A entails sentence B and sentence B is neutral with respect to A). We also analyzed some of the reasons for the wrong annotations. In the current work, we look at contradictions, since detecting conflicting or contradictory statements is a fundamental text understanding task within many applications, see Condoravdi et al. (2003). We started by looking the contradiction annotations which are asymmetric.

If proposition A is contradictory to B, then B must be contradictory to A. This is not what happens with these 611 pairs of SICK. From our processing of the corpus[2] we have the following asymmetric pairs:

- 8 pairs $AeBBcA$, meaning that A entails B, but B contradicts A;
- 327 pairs $AcBBnA$, meaning that A contradicts B, but B is neutral with respect to A;
- 276 pairs $AnBBcA$, meaning that A is neutral with respect to B, but B contradicts A.

These 611 asymmetric, problematic pairs, out of 9840 may seem few (around 6%) but given that the sentences were chosen to describe simple, non-abstract, common-sense situations, the number raises questions. We looked into these pairs and tried to analyze the reasons they were annotated as such and correct them, re-annotating them in a way that would make them symmetric and logical.

3 Observed mistakes

First of all, we discovered that some pairs contain ungrammatical sentences, e.g., *The black and white dog isn't running and there is no person standing behind.* Although the grammatical errors can be considered small, we can assume that each annotator mentally fixes the grammar in a different way, thus creating different relations and annotations. In this example, we could add an *it* at the end of the sentence or remove *behind* altogether and depending on this decision the sentence may have a different implicative behavior. There is also the case of nonsensical sentences in the corpus, e.g., *A motorcycle is riding standing up on the seat of the vehicle*, (did they just forget the word *driver* after *motorcycle*?) over which it is hard to reason – for the annotators and for us.

Additionally, there are sentences among the 611 pairs that simply seem wrongly annotated. We could not tell what was the reason for the wrong label. The pair A = *The blond girl is dancing behind the sound equipment.* B = *The blond girl is dancing in front of the sound equipment*, was marked as A contradicts B and B is neutral with respect to A. We should be talking about the same blond girl which is either in front or behind the sound equipment, for the same observer. Thus, B should also contradict A. A possible explanation here might be the vagueness of the notion of entailment for a "lay person". The RTE (Recognizing Textual Entailment[3]) task defines entailment as "given two text fragments called "Text" (T) and "Hypothesis" (H), it is said that T entails H (T $\rightarrow$ H) if, typically, a human reading T would infer that H is most likely true" (Dagan et al. (2006)). The problem with the "a human reading" clause is that it leaves too much choice for annotators. Annotators might have been overcompensating for the "human reading", assuming that – for the example above – different observers were at play.

[2] Available at https://github.com/kkalouli/SICK-processing/tree/master/pairs.

[3] https://www.aclweb.org/aclwiki/index.php?title=Recognizing_Textual_Entailment.

Similarly a pair like A = *A black and white dog is carrying a small stick on the green grass.* B = *A black and white dog is carrying a huge stick on the green grass.* Assuming that we are talking about the same dog, it is clear that a stick cannot be small and huge at the same time for the same observer, but notions of smallness will vary according to observers, so maybe the annotators decided that the size of the stick was not important enough to establish a contradiction between sentences.

We were able to deal with these kinds of mistakes by excluding them altogether from our cleaned version of the corpus. However, the task was not as easy for the other 520 cases out of the 611, for which some design flaws in the corpus construction created much confusion for the annotators and for us. As Marelli et al. (2014) mention in their paper, within corpora dedicated to inference, there is a high proportion of neutral annotations because most sentences are not related through inference. Also there are many neutral stances because the sentences of many pairs contain indefinite determiners and the usual interpretation of indefinite determiners creates a new referent, every time one indefinite determiner is present. Thus we discovered two main flaws in the original corpus design and construction. Firstly, when a picture is captioned most people use indefinites to introduce and describe the objects in the discourse. But this was not taken into consideration during the normalization process of the SICK sentences. This led to sentences with indefinites being paired with other sentences with indefinites. Such pairs are of course problematic due to the lack of a common reference. Secondly, the annotators were not given any guidelines on referents to judge the pairs and thus they tended to mark such pairs as neutral as the indefinite determiners were not binding to each other. An example is the pair: A= *A fearful little boy is on a climbing wall.* B= *A fearful little boy is on the ground.* Since there was no reason to assume that the indefinite little boys were the same, the annotators assumed that A and B are neutral with respect to each other because the two sentences can be talking about different *little boys*. If the sentences were talking about the same boy, they could not be true at the same time, so one would have a contradiction. But since the determiners are indefinite and there is no common referent, it is assumed that there were different boys.

Our investigation showed us that this phenomenon of "indefiniteness" and the lack of a specific context or reference created many other faulty annotations and not only the neutral ones already mentioned by Marelli et al. (2014).

4 Possible solutions

The previous literature in detecting and classifying contradictions in text is not very extensive. Previous works (Zaenen et al. (2005); de Marneffe et al. (2008)) argue that the events or entities of a sentence pair need to be coreferent if the pair is to be deemed a contradiction. Since the coreference of entities and events in the SICK pairs is not guaranteed, we could agree to take the sentences with indefinite determiners as they are and re-annotate them accordingly: the indefinite determiners in the example above would mean that the two boys are/can be different boys and therefore that the sentences should be marked neutral to each other. Although such an approach might feel natural and straightforward, it does not make a very useful contribution to the correction of the asymmetric annotations. This is because most pairs will get to be marked neutral by assuming independence of referents and events. This is due to the fact that if there is no binding referent, contradictions can only work if sentence A uses an indefinite determiner and B ultimately negates this with a universal quantifier, like *there is no*, *nobody*, *nothing*, etc. Other than that, the sentences ought to be reasonably similar. An example is the pair A = *There is no man chopping a log with an axe.* B = *A man is chopping a tree trunk with an axe.* But such constructions are not very common. In all other cases the pairs would have to be classified as neutral. We also did not consider good practice changing the determiners of those problematic sentences to definite ones. While this would avoid the existential quantification of the indefinites, this way we would be interfering with the corpus itself, changing it into something that is not the SICK corpus anymore.

Therefore, another kind of solution was necessary to correct these asymmetric annotations to something useful and reasonable. After considering different options, we concluded that the best way to correct the pairs would be to make a hard compromise: to try to *assume* that the pairs are talking about the same event and entities no matter what definite or indefinite markers are involved, with some restrictions, though. To assume that the entities and the events are coreferent is not so easy, especially in cases where the two sentences are very distant from each other in meaning. Therefore, we could only correct using this method the sentences of the pairs that are of an *atomic* nature, meaning the ones with only one predicate-argument structure. Those are easier to compare, if we assume coreference. If we try to correct the pair A = *There is no man singing and playing the guitar.* B = *A man is playing a guitar.* we have the problem that A is not atomic (there are two predicates) and therefore A is not analogous to B where we just have one predicate. In other words, even if we assume that the two men are the same, we still cannot fully compare the two sentences because if there is no man *singing AND playing the guitar* it does not mean that there is also no man just *playing the guitar*. Thus, the two sentences would get to be neutral in the sense that they are incomparable according to our criteria. On the contrary, if we have the pair A = *A man is getting off the car.* B= *A man is getting into a car.*, we just have *atomic* sentences and – assuming coreference – we can compare them easily to one another; we can make the man and the event coreferent and mark the pair as a contradiction since the same man cannot be getting in and off the car at the same time.

Apart from this first constraint – **i.** "one predicate-argument structure constraint" – there is another one we have to take into account, namely that **ii.** even sentences with *atomic* structures have to be close enough in meaning. It is one thing to make the – linguistically bad – compromise that we do not consider the semantic contribution of definite and indefinite determiners, that we say we only care to mark the entities and predicates present in the sentences. But it is another thing to also make the – logically and semantically bad – compromise that all entities corefer *no matter what is said about them*. If the two sentences are not as close in meaning, it is hard to assume coreference and therefore the sentences are incomparable for our purposes. If we take the pair A = *A man is eating a banana.* B= *The man is not eating a banana by a tree.*, it is hard to assume that the men are the same, although both sentences are *atomic*, because the man in B is *by a tree* which means that the sentence is not comparable with A where we do not know where the man is. On the contrary, if we have the pair A= *A large green ball is missing a potato.* B= *A large green ball is hitting a potato.*, we can easily assume that the large green ball is the same in both sentences and that it can either be missing or hitting the same potato at the same time, so the pair is a contradiction. Of course, this notion of "close enough meaning" is very hard to pin down and might vary from annotator to annotator. For our purposes of calibrating our annotations, we first commonly corrected the same pairs of the 611 in order to be sure that our way of seeing "closeness" is similar enough.

Although this method of correcting the asymmetrical annotations does make some serious compromises, it seemed to us the best one for the task at hand. No other method would give us a satisfactory result without altering the corpus too much or turning all asymmetrical pairs to neutral stances. Making all pairs neutral would mean that the useful pairs of the corpus would shrink even more – they are already less than half of all pairs. Of course, with our approach we also lose some of the pairs because they get to be *incomparable* but there seems to be no way out. Despite our linguistic compromises, our approach follows de Marneffe et al. (2008) who say that "contradiction occurs when two sentences are extremely unlikely to be true simultaneously" , a definition that attempts to "more closely match human intuitions". It seems plausible to assume that if an annotator has a pair of sentences that could be understood as talking about the same referents and about the very same event, that annotator would assume the coreference.

5 Taxonomy of mistakes

All in all, we find four kinds of mistakes within the asymmetrical pairs. First, there are ungrammatical sentences and we can assume that those mistakes come from the generation process of the pairs; some of the transformations did not work as expected. Secondly, we have the non-sensical pairs which again must have arisen during some of the automatic transformations. Both these mistakes have probably led the annotators to mentally fix them in different ways, thus creating asymmetrical annotations. Thirdly, we have discovered asymmetrical annotations that are plain errors for which we cannot say much about the source of the mistakes. Lastly, there are mistaken annotations due to the lack of a common reference and the presence of indefinites. The flaws in the corpus design and construction could probably account for those mistakes. We would like to stress at this point that we cannot give any quantitative measures of these mistakes as many sentences belong to more than one of these categories and thus we cannot classify the mistakes absolutely.

6 Conclusions

What we concluded is that for our purpose of creating a textual inference system but also more generally, for the purpose of creating inference corpora such as SICK, the explicitation of the referents of a sentence plays an important role, especially when dealing with contradictions. This explicitation is called the grounding of a sentence in Bowman et al. (2015), for instance. Whether creating a corpus or building an inference system, the creators of a corpus should make sure that there are specific referents on which the sentences are judged or grounded. On the one hand, for the creation of a corpus we suggest two such control mechanisms. Firstly, the creators could make the referents explicit by showing to the annotators the pictures from which the captions come and instructing them to judge the pairs according to the pictures and only them. However, such methods with pictures restrict the kind of language and information that can be conveyed and detected to concrete and literal actors and events. Other types of reference assigning, e.g. using Skolem constants as in Bobrow et al. (2007), can be tried out as well. Secondly, the corpus creators could employ other data collection methods (e.g. everyday conversations about concrete people) apart from captions' descriptions as these are bound to such problems as it was explained before. If it is deemed necessary to stick to pictures, the design of the collection could still be improved by providing the picture and asking the subjects to only finish off the captions which already introduce the referents of discourse so that no multiple referents are introduced by the subjects, e.g. *The woman is....* Moreover, if captions are the chosen way, a normalization step could make sure that such phenomena of indefiniteness disappear. On the other hand, inference systems should contain an extra pre-processing step where the sentences are compared for *predicate-argument structure similarity* or, in other words, for frames of coreference, so problematic cases like the ones presented above would not enter the inference engine at all.

A manual investigation and correction of these asymmetric pairs seems an important step in "healing" SICK so that we can use it for testing a semantic pipeline. Any pipeline that aims at extracting semantic representations from sentences and using those representations for entailment and contradiction detection in a logic-enforcing way needs to have symmetric contradictions. The entailments detected might be relaxed later on, to hold up to probabilities or up to likelihood only, but uncontroversial cases should be made explicit to begin with.

7 Future work

We hope to devise less expensive mechanisms for verifying the rest of the corpus, making use of lexical and knowledge resources. In particular we started a small experiment where we automatically filter out the pairs that are only one-word apart. This will allow us to see how many of these are easy entailments (e.g. *A = The snowboarder is leaping fearlessly over white snow. B = The snowboarder is leaping over white snow*), how many are easy contradictions (e.g. *A= A deer is jumping over a fence. B=A deer isn't jumping over the fence.*), how many we need to declare neutral. The hope is to come up with mechanisms for the construction of logic-based corpora that can be easily extended via composition, to serve as stringent baselines for hybrid logic-linguistic and machine learning systems.

References

Beltagy, I., S. Roller, P. Cheng, K. Erk, and R. J. Mooney (2015). Representing meaning with a combination of logical form and vectors. *CoRR abs/1505.06816.*

Bobrow, D. G., C. Condoravdi, R. Crouch, V. de Paiva, L. Karttunen, T. H. King, R. Nairn, L. Price, and A. Zaenen (2007). Precision-focused textual inference. In *Proceedings of the ACL-PASCAL Workshop on Textual Entailment and Paraphrasing*, pp. 16–21. Association for Computational Linguistics.

Bowman, S. R., G. Angeli, C. Potts, and C. D. Manning (2015). A large annotated corpus for learning natural language inference. *arXiv preprint arXiv:1508.05326.*

Condoravdi, C., D. Crouch, V. De Paiva, R. Stolle, and D. G. Bobrow (2003). Entailment, intensionality and text understanding. In *Proceedings of the HLT-NAACL 2003 workshop on Text meaning-Volume 9*, pp. 38–45. Association for Computational Linguistics.

Dagan, I., O. Glickman, and B. Magnini (2006). The PASCAL recognizing textual entailment challenge. In *Proceedings of the PASCAL Challenges Workshop Recognizing Textual Entailment.*

de Marneffe, M.-C., A. N. Rafferty, and C. D. Manning (2008). Finding contradictions in text. In *Proceedings of ACL-08.*

Kalouli, A.-L., L. Real, and V. de Paiva (to appear, 2017). Textual inference: getting logic from humans. In *Proceedings of the 12th International Conference on Computational Semantics (IWCS).*

Marelli, M., S. Menini, M. Baroni, L. Bentivogli, R. Bernardi, and R. Zamparelli (2014). A SICK cure for the evaluation of compositional distributional semantic models. In *Proceedings of LREC 2014.*

Zaenen, A., L. Karttunen, and R. Crouch (2005). Local textual inference: can it be defined or circumscribed? In *Proceedings of the ACL workshop on empirical modeling of semantic equivalence and entailment*, pp. 31–36. Association for Computational Linguistics.

Identifying Polysemous Words and Inferring Sense Glosses in a Semantic Network

Maxime Chapuis
ENSIMAG
maxime.chapuis@ensimag.fr

Mathieu Lafourcade
LIRMM
mathieu.lafourcade@lirmm.fr

Introduction

The present paper aims at detecting polysemous words from their hypernyms. For instance, a native speaker knowing that the French word *frégate* (*frigate*) is a *ship* and a *bird* can easily guess that *frégate* is polysemous. Indeed, it is difficult to conceive something being both a *ship* and a *bird* at the same time. We can say that those two hypernyms are *"incompatible"*. If one had a list of all incompatible hypernyms (which will be referred as *incompatibility rules* later in this paper), one could easily detect polysemous words. Is it possible to create such a list ? Can it be done automatically ? To answer these questions we experimented on the French lexical-semantic network JeuxDeMots, Lafourcade (2007), which a free and open resource.

Identifying polysemous words is crucial in order to understand a text. It is usually done by detecting high density components in co-occurrence graphs created from large corpora, as in Véronis (2003). Similar methods have been used by Dorow and Widdows (2003) and Ferret (2004) to discover word senses also in corpora. To detect the different dense areas of their graphs, Dorow and Widdows (2003) used the Markov Cluster Algorithm, van Dongen (2000). These methods are very effective, but they highly depend on the corpora used to create the graphs which might induce many biases. To choose the proper glosses for naming the different word senses, Dorow and Widdows (2003) used the hypernyms present in the lexical network WordNet, Fellbaum (1998). WordNet is also used by Ferret (2004) to evaluate his results. We experimented our approach on the French lexical-semantic network JeuxDeMots, and there is no other complete enough french resources equivalent to WordNet to automatically compare our results to. Hence, we had to rely on some manual evaluation.

In this paper, we will first present the JeuxDeMots network and some of its specificities. Then, we will detail the method we used (a) for generating list of incompatible hypernym and then (b) for inferring glosses for naming word senses, followed by some evaluations.

1 Methods for Dealing with Incompatibilities and Glosses

1.1 Few Aspects of the JeuxDeMots Lexical-Semantic Network

JeuxDeMots (JDM), Lafourcade (2007) is a French lexical-semantic network. It is a knowledge base containing lexical and semantic information. The network is composed of terms (nodes) and relations (edges). The relations between nodes are typed, oriented and weighted. Around 100 relation types are defined, such as synonymy, antonymy, generic (hypernymy), specific (hyponymy) and refinements. Refinements are representations of word senses or usages.

The different refinements of a given term T take the form of (T, glosses) pairs, as T>$glose_1$, T>$glose_2$, ..., T>$glose_n$. Glosses are terms that help the reader to identify the proper meaning of T. For instance, the French term *frégate* (*frigate*), which is a *ship* and a *bird*, has two refinements, *frégate>navire* and *frégate>oiseau*. Thus, a term T is linked to its refinements in the network, through a specific relation type (*r_semantic_raff*).

1.2 Generating Incompatibility Rules

The algorithm used to generate the rules relies on the *refinements* present in JDM to partition sets of hypernyms (there are around 26 000 refined terms and more than 69 000 refinements in the network).

Let **T** be a refined term of JDM with two refinements **A** and **B**. Suppose that **T** has only two hypernyms and that one is a hypernym of **A** and the other a hypernym of **B**. Partitioning the hypernyms of **T** is trivial because you only have to put one hypernym in a partition and the other in a different partition.

Let's go further and assume that **A** and **B** have now multiple hypernyms. The algorithm still creates two partitions but this time, it selects among the hypernyms of **T**, every hypernym *h* which is only in **A** or only in **B**, and puts it in the corresponding group. These groups can be expressed as:

$$\begin{aligned} G_A &= \{h \in hypernyms(T) \wedge h \in hypernyms(A) \wedge h \notin hypernyms(B)\} \\ G_B &= \{h \in hypernyms(T) \wedge h \notin hypernyms(A) \wedge h \in hypernyms(B)\} \end{aligned} \tag{1}$$

This process can be generalised to n sets of hypernyms. Let's assume now that **T** has n refinements R_1, R_2, ..., R_n, then the algorithm selects among the hypernyms of **T**, every hypernym h which is only present in one refinement and creates the corresponding groups. The previous expression becomes:

$$\forall j \neq i, \quad G_{R_i} = \{h \in hypernyms(T) \wedge h \in hypernyms(R_i) \wedge h \notin hypernyms(R_j)\} \tag{2}$$

This algorithm gives us a way to group the hypernyms of **T**. Let's run it on an example:

```
hypernyms(T)  = {a, b, c, d, e, f}
hypernyms(R1) = {a, b, c, g}
hypernyms(R2) = {a, d, h}
hypernyms(R3) = {e, f, i, j}
```

GR1 = {b, c}   GR2 = {d}   GR3 = {e, f}

The hypernym *a* is present in both R_1 et R_2, therefore it is ignored (it does not meet the condition (2)). The hypernyms *b* and *c* are both hypernyms of **T** and are only in the refinement R_1, thus they end up in the group corresponding to R_1. It goes the same way for *d*, *e* and *f* which are only in R_2 and R_3. The hypernyms *g*, *h*, *i* et *j* are ignored because they are not hypernyms of **T**.

The hypothesis we made is that, if for a term **T** with n senses the algorithm produces the groups G_1, G_2, ..., G_n, the hypernyms of a group are *incompatible* with the hypernyms of all the other groups, meaning that for $i \neq j$:

$$\forall x \in G_i, \forall y \in G_j, \quad x \quad incompatible \quad y \tag{3}$$

The generated rules are represented as:

```
hypernym1|hypernym2|origin|GroupID1|GroupeID2
```

where :

- *hypernym1* and *hypernym2* are two incompatible hypernyms ;
- *origin* is the refined term used to generate the rule ;
- *GroupID1* (resp. *GroupID2*) is a unique integer identifying the group where *hyperonyme1* (resp. *hyperonyme2*) belongs.

Here is an example of a rule:

```
n1="papillon>insecte"|n2="oiseau>animal"|origin="empereur"|gId1=2192|gId2=2191
```

The hypernym *papillon>insecte* (*butterfly>insect*) is *incompatible* with *oiseau>animal* (*bird>animal*). The rule was generated using the term *empereur* which in French is both the name of a *butterfly* and the name of a *bird*. The hypernym *papillon>insecte* belongs to the group 2192 and *oiseau>animal* to the group 2191. The group identifiers will be used later in section 1.4 to choose the right glosses of the refinements.

However, you should proceed with caution when using this method because the JDM network is not complete yet. It contains many silences[1] which could lead to the production of false rules. Let's take the example of the French term *aubergine* (*eggplant*) and its two refinements "*aubergine>plante potagère*" (*eggplant*) and "*aubergine>contractuelle*" (*policewoman*) :

```
hypernyms(aubergine) = {plante, femme, personne, eucatyote, etre vivant}
hypernyms(aubergine>plante potagere) = {plante, eucaryote, etre vivant}
hypernyms(aubergine>contractuelle) = {femme, personne, etre vivant}
```

If you follow the algorithm as it was presented, you will produce the following rules : *plante incompatible femme*, *plante incompatible personne*, *eucaryote incompatible femme*, *eucaryote incompatible personne*. The absence of *eucaryote* (*eukaryote*) in the hypernyms of *aubergine>contractuelle* leads the the production of two false rules (*eucaryote incompatible femme* and *eucaryote incompatible personne*). One solution to the problem would be to add the hypernym *eucaryote* to *aubergine>contractuelle*. However, the fact that a *policewoman* is a *eukaryote* seems to be irrelevant even if ontologically true.

Another solution is to intentionally ignore the hypernyms which are high in the hierarchy. For instance *être vivant(living being)* or *métazoaire* (*metzoan*) seem too general to give us useful information. Therefore, the algorithm uses a list of around 50 hypernyms to ignore such as *biconte (bikont), uniconte (unikont), chose (thing)*, *organisme (organism), etc.* .

1.3 Checking Produced Rules

Despite the previous filtering, the list of rules still contains false or non-productive rules. A rule is considered *valid* if there are at least two examples to back it up and *productive* if it produces at least one result. This is a way to remove rules that are too specific from the list. For each rule (*A incompatible B*), the algorithm searches in the network the terms which have both A and B as hypernyms. Let x be a term having A and B as hypernym. If x is already refined in JDM, x is considered as an *example* of the rule and will be used to validate it (there is at least one example to each rule: the term used to generate it). If x is not refined, it is considered as a *result* of the rule.

We have noticed that rules which have more *results* than they have *examples* tend to be false, therefore they are not validated by the algorithm. Being restrictive when validating the rules is not really a problem. Since they are created in groups (cf section 1.2), there is some redundancy in the list, the results of the rules created from the same groups usually overlap.

Another criteria we used to validate a rule, is that A should not be a hypernym of B and B should not be a hypernym of A, otherwise the rule is most likely false. For instance, the rule "*félin (feline) incompatible mammifère (mammalian)*" is false because a *feline* is a *mammalian*.

At the end of this process, we end up with a list of validated rules. The results of these rules are annotated as "to refine or to correct". Indeed, a term can be detected as polysemous because of an incorrect relation of hypernymy. Therefore the results should be double-checked by an expert. The results are stored as: the term detected polysemous, followed by the rules violated by the term. Here is an example of result for the term *danois*:

```
danois
n1="mammifere"|n2="langue"|origin="mangue"|gId1=1342|gId2=1340
n1="mammifere carnivore"|n2="langue>75266"|origin="persan"|gId1=10767|gId2=10765
n1="langue>75266"|n2="animal>117095"|origin="mara"|gId1=919|gId2=918
n1="langue>75266"|n2="mammifere"|origin="mara"|gId1=919|gId2=918
```

In this example, *danois* has been detected as polysemous because in French this term refers to both the Danish language and a dog breed.

1.4 Choosing Glosses

To further automate the process, we created an algorithm capable of finding the glosses of a refinement in most cases. The idea is to use the rules violated by a word to find the different glosses. Let

[1] A silence is the absence of a relation which should be present between two terms

$R_1, R_2, ...R_n$ be the rules violated by the term T. It is possible, thanks to the group identifiers previously created (see section 1.2), to reconstruct groups of hypernyms. Thus, the hypernyms of the R_i rules are grouped by their group identifiers. These *"local"* groups (*"local"* because they are created using the rules of a specific result) are called the L_i. If we apply this to the example *danois*, we find the following L_i groups:

$$\begin{aligned} L_{1342} = \{\textit{mammifère}\}, L_{919} = \{\textit{langue>langage}\}, L_{10767} = \{\textit{mammifère carnivore}\} \\ L_{10765} = \{\textit{langue>langage}\}, L_{1340} = \{\textit{langue}\}, L_{918} = \{\textit{mammifère, animal>zoologie}\} \end{aligned} \tag{4}$$

Applying the same process to the entire list of rules gives you back the groups initially created in section 1.2. These *"general"* groups (*"general"* because they are created using every rule of the list) are called the the G_i. The G_i groups give information about the L_i groups, especially which of the L_i groups can be merged together. When creating the G_i groups, if a group contains a refinement, we decided to add the general term of said refinement to the group. We obtain the following G_i groups for the example *danois*:

$$\begin{aligned} G_{1342} = \{\textit{mammifère}\}, G_{919} = \{\textit{langue, langue>langage}\} \\ G_{10767} = \{\textit{mammifère carnivore, carnivore, félin, mammifère}\} \\ G_{10765} = \{\textit{langue, langue>langage}\}, G_{1340} = \{\textit{langue}\} \\ G_{918} = \{\textit{mammifère, animal, animal>zoologie, rongeur}\} \end{aligned} \tag{5}$$

Because of the way they are created, we have the following relation between the L_i and the G_i:

$$\forall i, \quad \textit{GroupID}(L_i) = \textit{GroupID}(G_i) \quad \textit{and} \quad L_i \subseteq G_i \tag{6}$$

After that, the algorithm merges the "*local*" groups which have an intersection with the "*general*" groups different from null. For instance, if $(L_{1342} \cap G_{918}) \neq \emptyset$, it merges L_{1342} and L_{918}. The merge of the groups can be written as:

$$(L_i \cap G_j \neq \emptyset) \Rightarrow \textit{merge}(L_i, L_j) \tag{7}$$

When applying this process to the example *danois*, the algorithm merges its L_i into two groups:

$$\begin{aligned} L_{10767} = \{\textit{mammifère carnivore, mammifère, animal>zoologie}\} \\ L_{10765} = \{\textit{langue>langage, langue}\} \end{aligned} \tag{8}$$

Finally, the algorithm selects in each group the hypernym which has the biggest weight in the network. These hypernyms are used as glosses of the refinements of **T**. For the term *danois*, the algorithm suggests the refinement "*danois>mammifére*" (*mammalian*) for the dog breed, and the refinement "*danois>langue*" (*language*) for the Danish language. The glosses found by the algorithm are not always as accurate as the ones that a human would give, but they are usually true.

2 Results and Discussion

With this method, we created 25 119 rules, 2 785 of which have been validated. With these rules, our system identified 3 171 words as polysemous. To assess the precision of these results, we conducted two experiments. The first one aims to evaluate the performances of the detection of polysemous words. To do that, we selected a sample of 320 terms identified as polysemous, and we checked every term manually (it represents 10% of all the words identified) (see table 1).

Correctly identified	False positive	Precision	Error
285	35	89%	11%

Table 1: Precision of the identification of polysemous words on a 320 terms sample

False positives are either due to incorrect rules or to errors in the network. Indeed, if a term has incorrect hypernyms, the term might be identified as polysemous, even if it is not. However, false positives are interesting because finding and correcting them can help to increase the overall network's accuracy.

The false negatives are all the unrefined polysemous words of JDM that were not identified as such. False negatives can happen when the words do not have enough hypernyms or when the system does not have the rules needed to identify them. Given the size of the network (more than 2 000 000 terms and 100 000 000 relations) it is difficult to explore the network manually in order to find the number of false negatives. It is important to note that this method is best used on nouns and named entities because adjectives and verbs tend to have fewer hypernyms than nouns and therefore are less susceptible to produce good results.

The goal of the second experiment was to test the accuracy of the inferred glosses. To do so, a sample of 300 polysemous words was selected. The glosses were then sorted in two categories. They were either considered "Correct", meaning that the system found one appropriate gloss for each discovered senses, or considered "Ambiguous or Inaccurate", meaning that the glosses found were too ambiguous to make the difference between the different senses, or that the system found to many glosses[2].

Correct	Ambiguous or Inaccurate
232	68
77%	23%

Table 2: Accuracy of inferred glosses on a 300 polysemous words sample

As you can see in table 2, the results are encouraging but the process of finding the glosses automatically still needs some improvements. It is not accurate enough yet to be used without a human verification. It is a quite difficult topic, and even when the glosses are "correct", they are less accurate than the glosses given by humans.

Conclusion

In this paper we have presented two approaches (a) to identify polysemous words in a lexical-semantic network, and (b) naming the discovered word senses by inferring adequate glosses. The results obtained on the JeuxDeMots network are promising as they both contributed to the network refinement and to the increase of its accuracy by detecting potential errors.

A possible improvement, if computation time is not critical, could be to enhance the precision of the glosses by selecting terms that are the most connected in the neighbourhood in the network instead of just choosing the term which weight is the highest.

References

Dorow, B. and D. Widdows (2003). Discovering Corpus-Specific Word Senses. *EACL 2003, pp. 79-82.*

Fellbaum, C. (1998). *WordNet: An Electronic Lexical Database*. Bradford Books.

Ferret, O. (2004). Découvrir des sens de mots à partir d'un réseau de cooccurrences lexicales. *TALN 2004.*

Lafourcade, M. (2007). Making people play for Lexical Acquisition with the JeuxDeMots prototype. In *7th International Symposium on Natural Language Processing (SNLP'07).*

van Dongen, S. (2000). A cluster algorithm for graphs. *Technical Report INS-ROOl 0, National Research Institute for Mathematics and Computer Science, Amsterdam, The Netherlands, May..*

Véronis, J. (2003). Cartographie lexicale pour la recherche d'information. *TALN 2003, pp. 265-274.*

[2]It is the case when the system fails to properly merge the groups. As a result, it proposes more glosses than the word have senses.

AUTHOR INDEX